TALES OF OLD
AIREDALE
A Miscellany

Ten true stories of Bradford and
Airedale's lost places, forgotten history,
eccentric heroes and unsolved mysteries

LISA FIRTH

First published November 2014
This edition February 2024

ISBN 979-8879385502

British Library Cataloguing in Publication Data.
A catalogue record for this book is available from the British Library.

Cover design, editing and typesetting by Fully Booked Design:
fullybookeddesign.co.uk

Contents

Map of Bradford and Airedale

© OpenStreetMap contributors

Important Locations: Map Key

(Locations are approximate)

1. Saltaire and Salts Mill

2. Shipley Glen, where Milner Field house was located

3. Hewenden Mill, workplace of John Nicholson when he published his bestselling book of poetry

4. Cottingley, site of the fairy photograph hoax

5. Thackley, birthplace of Joseph Wright

6. Goit Stock woods and waterfall

7. Bolling Hall, Bradford (now a historical museum)

8. Site of the Exley Head Workhouse, home of John Sagar

9. Apperley Bridge, where Prophet Wroe was baptised in the River Aire

10. Bilton Place, home of James Berry

Salts Mill in 1859 (above) and today (below; © Mark Jankowski)

Bradford's New Eden

Sir Titus Salt and his model village, Saltaire, saved the lives of thousands of Bradford workers – at a price.

. . . .

SALTAIRE, a model village in golden sandstone nestling on the banks of the River Aire, had long been known as one of Bradford's hidden treasures before its designation as a UNESCO World Heritage Site in 2001 brought it to international attention. Today the village attracts thousands of visitors every year from around the globe, and it has also found fame on stage and screen. In 2010 the BBC's *South Riding* was

Sir Titus Salt

filmed in the village, and more recently a 2013 episode of *Doctor Who*, 'The Crimson Horror', featured a fictional village based on Saltaire. (Although the episode itself was filmed in Caerphilly, a near-perfect copy of Salts Mill appeared courtesy of CGI – long gone are the days when special effects on *Doctor Who* meant tinfoil trousers and toilet plungers!)

Unlike Diana Rigg's villainous mill owner in 'The Crimson Horror', however, the real Sir Titus wasn't in the habit of pickling his workers in crimson venom. (In fact, his fear of his people being 'pickled' is well-known – Salt famously refused to allow any pubs to be built in Saltaire. There are a few watering holes in the village these days though, including the aptly-named Don't Tell Titus.) Thankfully, the real story of Titus Salt's New Jerusalem is far less sinister.

When the 19-year-old Titus moved to Bradford in 1822, it was a city undergoing rapid expansion: a population of 13,000 at the turn of the century had bloated to a staggering 104,400 by 1851. By the time Salt decided to build his model community, the so-called 'Worstedopolis' was a slum-ridden, unhealthy, overcrowded mess.

Bradford residents then had a life expectancy of just over 18. Sewage was dumped directly into the beck that provided the city's drinking water, and outbreaks of cholera and typhoid were frequent. Meanwhile, 200 factory chimneys pumped out a noxious mix of airborne poisons. Prior to the 1833 Factory Act, children as young as six could expect to be put to work in the mills for as many as 14 hours a day. More brothels graced the streets than churches, and alcoholism was common. It was a dirty, diseased and depressing existence.

Titus Salt's rapid ascent began in 1836 when he bought a consignment of unwanted Peruvian alpaca wool (a purchase later playfully satirised by Charles Dickens in his sketch 'The Great Yorkshire Llama'). It was believed alpaca wool could not be used for worsted manufacture, but Salt discovered that by binding with silk, a strong, lustrous material could be created. By 1850 he owned five mills and was one of the richest men in Yorkshire.

Despite his success, Salt was frustrated. He was elected Mayor in 1848, yet his attempts to improve living conditions were thwarted at every turn. Although he had introduced pollution-reducing burners into his own factories, he couldn't persuade the council to pass a bylaw forcing other mills to follow suit. Like tobacco companies in the 20th century, factory owners simply refused to acknowledge the inconvenient truth that their smoke was the cause of ill health.

Salt was then Bradford's biggest employer. Determined to improve life for his 3000 workers, in 1849 he marched into the office of architects Lockwood and Mawson (who later went on to design St George's Hall) and asked them to build him a mill.

Over the next 27 years, Salt constructed a model community with living conditions decades ahead of their time. The village was built four miles from Bradford in beautiful countryside, on land conveniently close to the river, canal and railway. With the Italianate mill as the focal point, Salt supervised the building of 824 neat terraced cottages for his workers, each with its own yard, toilet, water and gas supply, and with at least two bedrooms. Situated close to stunning Shipley Glen, Saltaire must have seemed a paradise after the pestilent Bradford slums.

Salt's ambitious vision didn't end with comfortable housing. To encourage cleanliness, he built wash-houses and public baths. He built a hospital, library, school and rent-free almshouses

It was said that Titus Salt built the congregational church, which he knew would be his final resting place, to face Salts Mill as a daily reminder of his mortality. His mausoleum can be seen behind the church on the left

for the old and infirm. He built an institute, billiard rooms, allotments, a gym and concert hall. In 1872 a riverside park was added, with leisure activities including band performances, archery and boating.

Salt was the first mill owner in Bradford to introduce a maximum ten-hour working day, and he provided a pension for the elderly 40 years before the first state pensions. His mill, too, was designed with workers' comfort in mind, producing less noise and cleaner emissions than any in Europe. The last building in Saltaire was completed in 1876. Having lived to see his great work completed, Titus Salt died later that same year.

Salt built a demi-utopia, but his workers paid a price for their escape from the slums. In a community of his own creation, the prince of industry became a dictator, albeit one with a philanthropic agenda. Exercising a father-knows-best paternalism that not only forbade drunkenness but also set down rigid rules about lifestyle, leisure and socialising (as well as banning trade unions), the stern, bearded disciplinarian must have seemed not unlike some Victorians' notion of God.

But his popularity never wavered. When he was interred at his beloved congregational church, now a Grade I-listed building, over 100,000 people lined the route of his coffin. It was the biggest funeral Bradford had ever seen.

He may have his detractors, but Sir Titus Salt offered his workers a better, cleaner, longer life at a time when poverty and early death were the norm. And it takes more than a sonic screwdriver to achieve that.

Saltaire Facts

✔ Saltaire is one of the best-preserved model villages still in existence. It was awarded UNESCO World Heritage Status in 2001.

✔ The Italianate chimney of 'New Mill', built to expand the existing mill in 1868, is based on the campanile of Sta Maria Gloriosa dei Frari in Venice.

✔ Salts Mill closed for business in 1986 and (thanks to the dedication of its buyer, Jonathan Silver) reopened the following year as an art gallery to display the works of local boy David Hockney. Entry to the 1853 Gallery is free: find out more at www.saltsmill.org.uk

✔ Events in the village include the Saltaire Arts Trail, which takes place every year in May, and a popular festival held in September (more details at www.saltairefestival.co.uk).

✔ The Salt family coat of arms can be seen on a number of buildings around Saltaire. The coat of arms consists of two stars with an ostrich motif, symbolising obedience and serenity. The family motto, emblazoned underneath, is Quid Non Deo Juvante – "what is not possible with God's help?"

✔ Titus Salt, always interested in improving the lot of his fellow man, had originally wanted to be a doctor but gave up this dream when he found he couldn't stand the sight of blood!

Saltaire's Pride

Were the stone lions of Saltaire meant for London's Trafalgar Square – and do they really come alive at night?

IN Saltaire's Victoria Square four lions are on guard, sitting regally atop their stone pedestals above the heads of visitors. The lion named Peace licks his paw in a wounded manner – perhaps from an injury caused by snarling War, sitting alongside and baring his teeth through the hanging chestnut leaves. Opposite sit another pair: ambitious Determination, holding himself proudly erect and staring loftily into the distance, and his brother Vigilance, ever on the alert, gazing up at the skies.

Determination the lion is said to roam Saltaire by night

London artisan Sir Thomas Milnes sculpted the four-strong
pride in rich Nidderdale sandstone for industrialist Titus Salt's
model village in 1868. The beasts are incredibly realistic, from
their luxurious curling manes right down to the velvet folds of
their slack hides – the sculptor based them on detailed sketches
he made of real-life counterparts at London Zoo. A visitor can
feel compelled to reach up and touch one of the heavy, powerful-
looking paws, half expecting to see a flicker of life (although
actually attempting to prod the lions awake may earn you an 'It
takes all sorts' eye-roll from a passing tourist, as I can testify from
personal experience!). It's no surprise at all to learn of a local
legend which says that every night when the church bells chime
12, the lions abandon their posts and go on the prowl, heading
down to the Aire for a drink.

The creatures' uncannily lifelike detail has been claimed as
the reason they don't have an even more prestigious (although
certainly no more beautiful) home than the one they have dwelt in
now for nearly 150 years. Several 19th-century accounts suggest
that the lions were originally intended for the base of Nelson's
Column in Trafalgar Square. However, following a disagreement
the commission was taken from Thomas Milnes and awarded
instead to Sir Edwin Landseer, who went on to produce the
bronze statues that still stand in the square today. According to
an urban myth, Milnes' sculptures were considered rather too –
ahem – anatomically correct for the prudish bigwigs of Victorian
London, who would make a dash for the nearest cold shower at
the sight of an uncovered piano leg, let alone an unneutered lion.

So the models supposedly remained in Milnes' showroom, where they were spotted by his old friend Sir Titus and requested for the outside of Saltaire's Factory School and the Mechanics' Institute (now Victoria Hall) opposite.

Wherever their home was originally intended to be, the lions are now synonymous with Saltaire. They've inspired the name of a local football team, been chosen as the subject of a "yarnbombing" knitting project during the Saltaire Arts Trail and even starred in their own calendar, created by a local photographer back in 2010.

The bronze lions of the capital may be better known, but it's doubtful they inspire more genuine admiration and affection than their four majestic Yorkshire cousins.

One of Landseer's lions in Trafalgar Square (© Jose L. Marin)

Salt's Ruin: The Curse of Milner Field

Like the skeletal shell of the once mighty Titanic lying desolate on the ocean bed, the sparse ruins of Titus Salt Jr's Milner Field mansion at Shipley Glen are steeped in history, legend – and a grim mythology.

· ·

IN November 1887, Titus Salt Jr – son and heir of his namesake, the Saltaire founder and self-made millionaire Sir Titus Salt – was relaxing in the billiard room of his luxurious mansion when he suddenly collapsed in pain. He was pronounced dead of heart failure shortly afterwards, aged only 44. This was just one in a series of bizarre tragedies to befall residents of Milner

Titus Salt Jr

Field, the sprawling estate Salt Jr had commissioned 18 years earlier.

There had been a time when it seemed as if the young businessman led a charmed life. Inheriting his industrialist father's vast textile empire following the latter's death in 1876, Salt was wealthy enough to have the world at his feet and this reputedly shy and reserved man found himself at the forefront of elite Yorkshire society. With his wife Catherine and their four

*Milner Field house pictured around 1885, two years
before Titus Salt Jr's premature death*

children, he played host to distinguished guests that included,
among others, the Prince and Princess of Wales (the future King
Edward VII and Queen Alexandra).

But the family's days of high living were soon to be at an end
as misfortunes came on thick and fast. A slump in the wool trade
deeply affected Salt's business affairs, further exacerbated by
unwise ventures in the United States and at home – he invested
money heavily in the lavish 1887 Yorkshire Jubilee Exhibition. In
addition, Salt's health had begun to fail: his doctor diagnosed a
weak heart in 1885, foreshadowing his death two years later.

The backdrop to Salt Jr's dramatic rise and fall was the
overwhelmingly extravagant, custom-built Milner Field mansion,

which replaced an older country house of the same name. A
Manderley-esque mass of turrets, towers and arches in neo-Gothic
Italianate style, the house boasted every luxury money could buy.

Nestled in beautiful wooded surroundings at Shipley Glen,
close to the Salt family wool empire in Saltaire, the estate featured
opulence on an unprecedented scale both inside and out, with
an orangery, courtyard, conservatory, boating lake and perfectly
landscaped gardens contained within its extensive grounds. Well
ahead of its time when completed in 1873, this estate agent's
dream included all mod cons: its own water supply, electricity
and sewage system, water-cooled refrigeration rooms and a direct

The Prince and Princess of Wales visit Milner Field, June 1882

telephone line to the mill at Saltaire.

After Salt Jr's death, Milner Field fell into the hands of Sir James Roberts, the new proprietor of Salts Mill, who purchased it from the late owner's widow. He too succumbed to the mansion's strange spell, and like his predecessor found himself beset by bad luck and personal calamities.

Roberts had already suffered the death of his eldest son from pneumonia in 1898. In 1904, the year he moved into Milner Field, this was followed by the tragic drowning of his 11-year-old youngest son during a family holiday in Ireland. His second son died of a nervous illness in 1912 aged 36, and Roberts' last surviving son, Harry, was badly injured in the First World War, preventing him from taking over the family business at Salts Mill as his father had hoped. The nurse Harry Roberts fell in love with while being treated for his injuries also died, pregnant with his child, in the flu epidemic that followed the war (Harry eventually married her sister, another nurse).

On top of these tragedies, the family were shamed by a national scandal when their married daughter's lover was murdered by her spouse in a notorious and widely-reported crime of passion. In 1903 Alice Roberts had eloped with a doctor, Norman Cecil Rutherford, greatly against her father's wishes: he had wanted her to wed another suitor, a Polish count. In 1919

The conservatory in a 1922 brochure (above), and as it is now (below)

Alice informed Norman – the father of her six children – that she wanted a divorce in order to marry her lover, his friend and colleague Major Miles Seton. Recently returned from tending wounded soldiers in the trenches and suffering from shell-shock, Dr Rutherford didn't take the news well. He hunted down his love rival Seton and put a bullet or three in his chest, spending ten years in Broadmoor for the crime.

Subsequent occupants of the estate also suffered tragic and often bizarre deaths. Ernest Gates lost his wife to a pre-existing illness just weeks after taking up residence in 1923, following her himself two years later after injuring his foot in a domestic accident and developing septicaemia. The exact cause of Ernest's injury is unknown, with rumours ranging from an unlucky scratch by a rose bush to an accidental whack with a golf club.

Milner Field's final owner, Arthur Remington Hollins, took the house in 1925 (like Ernest Gates before him, Hollins was a managing director of Salts Mill). His wife Anne died of pneumonia, aged only 43, less than a year after moving in, and three years later Arthur also passed away when he was suddenly taken ill during a summer holiday. Suffering from irritation of the gall bladder and diaphragm, Hollins literally hiccuped himself to death.

By the time of the Second World War the house had understandably acquired a macabre reputation, and that coupled with the cost of upkeep made it impossible to find a buyer for the once grand mansion. Having fallen into disrepair after two attempts to auction it off, Milner Field was used as a source of

Bricks from the house's bay window can still be seen at the site

building materials for repairs on Salts Mill. Derelict, gutted, roofless and with barely a trace of its former glory, the house was finally demolished in the 1950s – although an initial failed attempt to flatten the place with dynamite is testament to the quality of the original building work.

Visiting the site of Titus Salt Jr's once lavish estate today, it is tempting to recall the inscription on the ruined statue of the pharaoh Ozymandias in Percy Shelley's poem of that name:

And on the pedestal these words appear:

"My name is Ozymandias, king of kings:

Look on my works, ye Mighty, and despair!"

Nothing beside remains. Round the decay

Of that colossal wreck, boundless and bare

The lone and level sands stretch far away.

One wonders what Salt, an Ozymandias for his era, would make of the ruins of his sumptuous palatial home. All that now remains to testify to the vast estate's existence are a few piles of brick, some fragments of the conservatory's mosaic floor hidden in the undergrowth at Shipley Glen, and the ghosts that are said to wander the site.

Unsurprisingly given its gruesome history, there are stories of a number of spectral former inhabitants, with identities ranging from Salt Jr himself to Eva Gates and Anne Hollins, the wives of the final two owners. The most intriguing resident ghost must be an Edwardian figure known as 'The Green Man of Milner Field', who, it's claimed, first appeared to a local schoolboy in the 1950s. Dressed all in green, he roams the ruins playing on a flute.

Were the residents of Milner Field victims of an otherworldly curse, or simply prey to a series of unfortunate coincidences and the period's high mortality rates? Whatever the truth, the legend of this lost estate, reduced now to rubble and ashes, will live on.

I am indebted for much of the detail on Milner Field's history in this chapter to Richard Lee-Van den Daele and R David Beale's excellent book, *Milner Field: The Lost Country House of Titus Salt Jr*. For anyone interested in the estate, the book is available to buy online from www.milnerfield.co.uk

Milner Field library, 1885

The Bingley Byron

It's now over 170 years since the death of John Nicholson, "The Airedale Poet". Nicholson was a feted celebrity within his own lifetime, a Romantic poet from the ranks of the working classes. Yet now his lilting, melodic rhymes have been all but forgotten.

· ·

"OF all the Airedale-born poets, John Nicholson had the highest endowments of genius," Ethelbert Binns enthused in the 1892 *Wilsden Almanac*, 50 years after the poet's death. Nicholson's verses were a sell-out hit when they were published in 1824, running to two editions within months. His funeral attracted over a thousand mourners to Bingley churchyard. Yet now you could be forgiven for asking, "John who?".

Nicholson was born in Leeds in 1790, moving to Eldwick with his family at just a few weeks old. Here he received his early education from a man named Briggs, who kept a schoolhouse on the top of Ilkley Moor. Mr Briggs supplemented his income by making brooms, taking his scholars up onto the moor to repeat their lessons while they picked heather and ling for his bristles. It was here that Nicholson became smitten with the moors, a love affair that was to continue until the end of his life.

Young John was then sent to Bingley Grammar School to complete his education. He attracted the master Dr Hartley's attention as "a youth of great quickness of parts, as well as a liveliness of disposition" and made great progress in English composition. However, a year's schooling there was considered ample for a boy intended to follow in his father's footsteps as a worsted manufacturer, and at the age of 13 Nicholson was apprenticed as a woolsorter.

He did not relish the work, much preferring to read. The young man devoured any book he could lay his hands on, with Shakespeare, Milton and Pope his authors of choice.

He would often stay up reading into the early hours and be late to start his work. To prevent this distraction, his mother hid his supply of candles – but necessity begets invention. John took a mustard jar and filled it with the olive oil used for preparing wool, twisting a cotton rag for a wick. With this makeshift lamp, he was able to continue his late-night studies undeterred.

A skilful player of the hautboy, a type of oboe, it was while performing on this instrument at a wedding party that Nicholson first met Mary Driver. Mary and John married in July 1810, when he was just 19, but their happiness was tragically short-lived. In December of that year Mary died in childbirth, leaving John a widower with one child at the age of only 20.

The loss of his wife hit Nicholson hard. He swore to lead a more pious life from then on, and burying the symbol of his youthful indulgence, his hautboy, on the moor – where it probably remains – he became a Methodist lay preacher. The charismatic Nicholson drew large crowds and planned to train for the regular ministry.

This all changed when he met and married Martha Wild,

known affectionately as "Pat", in 1814. The Wesleyans were unimpressed at a second marriage so soon after his first wife's death, and Nicholson was debarred from the ministry.

The poet had a strong affection for both his wives. "I never loved, in the true sense of the word, but two," he told his brother in a sentimental mood, "and I married them both."

In 1818 he left his father's employment to work at Shipley Fields Mill. From there he moved to Harden Beck, and shortly after, to Hewenden Mill near Wilsden. Terminally unable to keep his mind on his job, another Hewenden worker recalled how Nicholson's pad-post and the whitewashed walls around were covered with his scribbles. He was also known to dot out his rhymes on the greasy surface of his sorting-board with a skewer.

It was here that he first gained celebrity as a poet. Nicholson had already made a name for himself as a satirist, circulating his almost libellous poetical sketches among friends. He achieved further fame in 1820 when he was commissioned by the manager of Bradford Old Theatre to write two dramatic works, *The Robber of the Alps* and *The Siege of Bradford*. These were performed with great success, reviving the fortunes of the struggling theatre. However, it wasn't until the publication of *Airedale in Ancient Times and other poems* in 1824 that Nicholson really became a household name. This volume was a bestseller, proving so popular that it ran to two editions within months. So sought after was it that people queued up to purchase sheets from the printers as they came off the presses, without even waiting for them to be bound!

John Nicholson, painted by his friend William Overend Geller

The publication was made possible by Nicholson's first patron, JG Horsfall, who had been impressed by his skill for off-the-cuff verse-making. Passing the poet's house one hot day, Horsfall asked for a drink of water and was obligingly given a glass of Nicholson's home-brewed ale instead. "Nicholson, they say you are a poet," said Horsfall jovially. "Let us hear what you can say about this pot of beer." Without stopping to think, the poet improvised:

> *O for an everlasting spring*
> *Of home-brew'd drink like this!*
> *Then with my friends I'd laugh and sing*
> *And spend the hours in bliss;*
> *Then come old Care, link'd with Despair,*
> *For I, with thee made strong,*
> *Would plunge them over head in beer,*
> *And make them lead the song.*

Horsfall became Nicholson's friend and champion, circulating his poems among gentlefolk and funding him as he worked on his volume of verses.

Nicholson had a real talent for impromptu poetry, and he would often use this skill to convince members of the gentry who doubted that the uncouth Yorkshireman was really the author of the verses they admired. On an occasion when he was asked to compose a poem on the freshly-drawn glass of porter in his hand, he rattled off this rhyme:

*View over Hewenden Valley, the area where Nicholson
worked while writing his bestselling volume of poetry*

The gallant, the gay and the sporter
Have here but little to stay;
For life's like the froth on that porter,
And quickly doth vanish away.

One poem, "The Poacher", was based on local men of his acquaintance. Intending to pen a verse on the subject, he befriended a notorious group of Wilsden pilferers and with these new friends would sit up at all hours, carousing in the name of research – much, it must be supposed, to the dismay of his family. Nicholson and his poacher friends had been known to polish off up to two gallons of the poet's home brew in just one sitting.

Two of these shady characters, Jack Moore and Dan Ingham, were the basis for the poachers Ignotus and Desparo in Nicholson's poem. Ingham once bragged that he had bagged enough game in his life to fill Hewenden Mill, and his mother was also notorious in the village, distilling moonshine whisky from her home in nearby Harecroft. Her house was known among the locals as a "whisht hoil" – a place for wanted felons to hide out.

Many of his poems were composed at majestic Goit Stock near where Nicholson worked. In summer he would rise at 4am and spend all day in this spot. Of his favourite haunt, he wrote:

Hail! Thou sequester'd rural seat,
Which ever beauteous dost appear,
Where the sweet songsters oft repeat
Their varied concerts, wild and clear!

Upon thy crystal-bosom'd lake
Th' inverted rocks and trees are seen,
Adorn'd with many a snowy flake,
Or in their leafy robes of green.

Here may the contemplative mind
Trace Nature and her beauties o'er
And meditation rest reclin'd,
Lull'd by the neighbouring cataract's roar.

[Extract from "Lines Written at Goit Stock", 1824]

The publication of *Airedale in Ancient Times* in 1824 marked a turning point in John Nicholson's career. Flushed with success, he gave up his job as a woolsorter and started making his living hawking his poems from door to door. However, always a heavy drinker, Nicholson's dependence on alcohol had by this time begun to spiral out of control. Much of the money raised through sales and the generous gifts of wealthy admirers at this period of his life may have been wasted on liquor.

His biographer John James, who was also a personal friend, hints at depression as the root of Nicholson's alcoholism. It's certain that he felt keenly his lack of formal education, and brooded much on this. "I will tell you what I am afraid of – many will compare my works with those who have had far greater privileges, and then they will be found wanting," the poet wrote once in a letter. Whatever the reason, Nicholson's dependence on drink became steadily more pronounced throughout his life, contributing eventually to his untimely end.

His addiction wasn't helped by his reputation for gregariousness: his witty remarks, improvised rhymes and practical jokes meant there were always those willing to stand him another drink in exchange for the pleasure of his company.

One anecdote of his drinking days, however, can't help but raise a smile. Nicholson patronised a local pub, where the landlady was excessively proud of her ancient punchbowl. She would often boast of its size, and wagered that if anyone could show her a larger, she would fill it with free drink for her customers. Relishing the challenge, Nicholson sought out an old stone baptismal font and had the basin delivered to the pub with his compliments. Tickled by the joke, the landlady set the punchbowl and the font side by side and filled them both for her patrons.

In 1827 he made a trip to London, intending to break into literary society there. The Yorkshireman certainly made quite an impression – but perhaps not for the reasons he had hoped. His biographer describes how he arrived in the capital with hair unkempt, in rustic blue coat, corduroy breeches and grey yarn stockings, and was considered rather a clownish bumpkin by the fashionable townies.

The visit wasn't a success. Nicholson soon got into a scrape when he fell in with some riotous young barristers, who one night took their new friend to the Drury Lane Theatre after a day's debauchery and abandoned him in the saloon there. He began drunkenly haranguing a bust of Shakespeare – quite what this much-admired idol had done to offend him is not known. This and his yokel-like appearance soon drew a mocking crowd, and Nicholson found himself the next day up before the beak for disorderly conduct. He escaped with a reprimand, but the press got hold of the story – "The Yorkshire Poet in trouble!" blazed the headlines. Afraid his wife might come and fetch him, Nicholson set off home.

A second visit to London, this time accompanied by Pat to keep him out of trouble, also failed to launch him into the capital's literary circle, although he had a few verses published. Sadly, during this visit he and his wife lost an infant child, a little girl named Martha – a tragic but all too common occurrence in Nicholson's time – and this forms the subject of one of his poems printed there.

His time as a wandering poet ended soon after this trip. Nicholson's publishers went bust, and many unsold copies of his work were seized and auctioned off at half price to pay their debts. The market for his poetry glutted, Nicholson was forced to once more look for work in the wool industry. He moved to Bradford in 1833, and there he remained for the rest of his life.

This was the final foil for Nicholson's once lofty ambition. He continued to write poetry, but alcoholism had affected his work and he never again scaled the dizzy heights of *Airedale*. Possibly his most notable writing during this period of his life came when he was commissioned to write some "hearts and minds" pieces raising awareness of the poor treatment of child workers in factories. Many young children were left permanently disabled by the cruelty, long hours and hard labour of the mills, and Nicholson composed an epic poem on the subject, "The Factory Child".

Nicholson spent the rest of his life working at Sir Titus Salt's warehouse in Bradford. Salt was an indulgent employer, turning a blind eye to the poet's irregular and poor-quality work as his drinking became more severe. Every holiday he would take himself off to the moors, "to clear his lungs of the Bradford smoke".

In 1836 he made one final effort to free himself from "the demon drink" when he signed the Temperance Pledge at the Wilsden Independent Chapel. He stated to the meeting that "he had been one of the most dreadful characters, and that perhaps he had drunk more liquor than any person present" – sounding something between a confession and a boast. Sadly, his commitment to abstinence lasted just 17 weeks before he fell back into old habits.

His family, eventually numbering nine children as well as his wife, were kept from absolute poverty during this time by some of the influential friends he had made earlier in his career. One friend, George Lane Fox, donated at least £200 to Nicholson's family both before and after the poet's death. Nicholson had been a frequent visitor to Fox's home and one of his poems, "Lines on Long Tom", is written to a drinking horn of that name possessed by Fox and capable of holding three pints of beer.

The Airedale poet met a sad end at the age of 52 when he

set out on the eve of Good Friday, 13th April 1843, to visit his widowed aunt in Eldwick. He never made it.

It was a stormy night and the Aire was violent and swollen. The poet "had made several stops on the way", as his Victorian biographer primly puts it, and had been well lubricated by the local alehouses by around midnight when he came to cross the stepping stones in what would later become Saltaire. Losing his footing, he was caught in the current and swept some way down the river. Although he managed to drag himself to the bank, he was too weak to move any further and was found dead of apoplexy the next morning. Rather aptly, his body was then laid out in a local pub while awaiting burial. Nicholson was buried in his beloved Bingley, his funeral attracting more than a thousand mourners.

So why has Bingley's feted woolsorter-wordsmith, of whom its people were once so proud, disappeared from among the ranks of Yorkshire's literary greats?

One explanation might be that Nicholson's florid, rhapsodic style just isn't appealing to a modern reader. Many of his poems are littered, even stuffed, with the classical allusions and sentimental, elaborate language of the Romantic school. He made no secret of his desire to find a market for his work among the gentry and clergy, and his poems are written in the vein most likely to impress this elevated group. It's also notable that there are no traces of dialect, no regional witticisms, even in his light-hearted pieces (although some of his rhymes give him away as a true son of the Dales – who but a Yorkshireman could make a couplet of "clear" and "there"?). For an Airedale man drawn from the ranks of the workers, the absence of any distinctively Yorkshire dialect and humour is really something of a disappointment.

Or maybe Nicholson's work has simply been out of print for too long – copies of his poems are now almost impossible to find anywhere other than the reference section of local libraries.

It seems a shame that Nicholson's work and reputation have all but vanished, as faults aside, some of his verses possess a charm beyond mere local interest. One such is an unpublished poem on the unlikely subject of the bursting of a peat bog near Haworth: a tripping, musical piece, and a fitting note on which to end his story.

What gigs what carts what marvelling hearts
Are pressing the mountain brown
To see a bog the valley clog
And in a deluge tumble down.
And as each flaw with greedy jaw
Quaft with unsatiated thirst
The lightnings flasht, the thunders crasht
And its tremendous bowels burst!

[Extract from "Lines on the bog bursting in Yorkshire", 1824.
Literary patriarch Patrick Brontë also wrote a poem about this
event, "The Phenomenon"]

Bingley Parish Church, where John Nicholson was laid to rest

*The grave of Mary Driver, Nicholson's first wife, in Bingley churchyard.
Nicholson's own headstone is thought to have been lost or removed,
along with many others, during the construction of a new road in 1904*

The Lost World of Goit Stock

The hidden beauty spot of Goit Stock, near Bingley, is considered by many to be a well-kept local secret. It's hard to believe now that this sleepy forest was once a thriving tourist resort, complete with menagerie, boating lake, dance hall and café.

....

POSITIONED somewhere between Harden, Wilsden and Cullingworth (and all three villages could rightfully lay claim to the area), Goit Stock is one of Airedale's best-kept secrets. Acres of gorgeous woodland reward the adventurous walker who wanders beyond peaceful Harden Park Homes caravan park, with the babbling beck guiding them to the site's jewel in the crown: a foaming, cacophonous 20-foot waterfall.

This serene landscape has served as the muse of many an artist, and is as inspiring today as it was in 1824 when the Airedale poet John Nicholson penned his "Lines Written at Goit Stock" (see pp25-26). It's hard to believe now that during the area's heyday in the Roaring Twenties, the gentle rush of the beck was drowned out by the chattering of monkeys and canaries, the oom-pahing of a brass band and the riotous merry-making of thousands upon thousands of joyful visitors...

Long after Nicholson's time, birdwatchers, tourists and ramblers started getting wise to this beauty spot tucked away between two textile mills. Flanked by Goit Stock Mill (which

stood on the site of what is now Harden Park Homes) at the one
end and Hallas Mill at the other, the woods and waterfall were the
perfect escape from industrialised Bradford and sightseers flocked
there in droves – much to the chagrin of the landowners, the
Ferrand family. They grumpily insisted that visitors to the woods
seek written permission before tramping all over their property.

By 1919, the Ferrands had realised that stemming the tide
of tourism was a lost cause and sold the woodland to a local
businessman. It was then that Goit Stock entered its golden age,
billed in the newspapers as "Happy Valley... the finest resort in
the North for pleasure parties".

Said to be "the pleasure resort of the poor man with a family",
the entry fee was just sixpence each for adults and threepence
for children, with discounts available for groups. "Charas'"
(motorised charabanc coaches) ran every half hour to and
from Bingley, packed with eager visitors, and at weekends and
holidays the site was often as crowded as Blackpool seafront.

An illustrated booklet of the early 1920s painted a picture of
the resort (in somewhat gushing terms):

> Goit Stock, with its two miles of gorgeous scenery, with ever-
> changing perspectives, its giant hills, peaceful vales, and majestic
> waterfalls – the light and shade of nature's glorious colourings – is
> indeed "a thing of beauty evermore".
>
> Here, "far from the madding crowd", one can rise with the sun and
> be greeted by the music of the songbirds, take their leisure during

the day, whilst at eventide —

"They can watch the big, husky sun wallow

In crimson and gold, and grow dim."

In those days the waterfall and woods were just the start of
Goit Stock's attractions. All sorts of leisure pursuits were on offer
for young and old alike. For animal lovers there was an aviary
and a monkey enclosure, as well as donkey and pony rides.
Sporty types could amuse themselves with rowing on the old mill
pond, enjoy game fishing, putting or clock golf, play cricket and
tennis, go bowling on the green, even have a boxing match! For
kiddies there were roundabouts and swings, a paddling pool and
a wooded toboggan run.

There was plenty to please music fans too. The cotton mill
had ceased spinning some time in the 1860s, making way for
spinning of a different kind as young sweethearts whirled around
the large ballroom on the second storey of the repurposed mill to
the swinging sound of the Goit Stock Orchestra, which played all
the latest dance hits. Outside, Wilsden Brass Band had their own
bandstand from which to entertain the crowds.

On high days and holidays, there were special events including
choral competitions, athletics meets, music festivals, gramophone
concerts, costume parties, firework displays and carnivals.

Many visitors packed up a picnic to eat in the woods, but for
those who preferred a more civilised lunch, a chintzy tearoom
on the top two floors of the converted Goit Stock Mill (above the
ballroom) could cater for over a thousand people. In addition, an

A picture postcard sent from Goit Stock in 1909

Majestic Goit Stock Waterfall as it is today

alfresco pavilion served tea on terraces overlooking dancing on the lawn, while kiosks dotted at convenient locations throughout the woods provided snacks and drinks to rambling parties.

Anyone having too much fun to even think about going home could purchase a bucket, bundle of sticks, matches and a mattress and stay under canvas overnight. However, those campers hoping to enjoy sleeping under the stars on the night of 18th April 1927 were not in for the serene evening they might have imagined...

On that day, Easter Monday, an estimated 20,000 people had thronged to the resort ready to make the most of the holiday and good weather. A special programme had been put on, the ballroom had been decked out with streamers and bunting, and dancing had continued right up until everything closed for the evening at 10pm.

All had seemed as it should be when the manager, James Dewhirst, locked up for the night, but less than two hours later a houseguest raised the alarm: huge flames could be seen lashing from the tearoom windows on both sides of the building. A stray cigarette end was later blamed for setting off the flammable decorations rigged up for the holiday.

Bingley Fire Brigade were called, but half an hour was all it took to gut the four-storey building. The blaze could be seen from as far away as Bingley, and as the fire engine rushed to the scene, the men saw the roof of the tearoom collapse – they knew then that the old mill was beyond salvation.

Nevertheless, the fire brigade battled valiantly to extinguish the flames. One officer ran dramatically through the blaze to

The tearooms (above) and bunting-decked dance hall (below)

gain access to a water supply. Another bravely climbed a flaming wooden staircase that was at imminent risk of collapse, sending a thrill through the watching crowd. The fire engine itself had to park so close to the blaze that it very nearly caught alight, and the heat was such that the building's glass windows melted and could be seen dripping down the walls.

By 3am the fire was out, but the building was a charred and blackened shell – and Goit Stock's glory days were gone forever.

Up to £10,000 of damage was done that night. Wilsden Band suffered a particularly heavy blow: music and instruments worth nearly £200 were lost in the fire, leaving them unable to fulfil their summer engagements. Members of the band hopefully trawled the wreckage next morning with picks and shovels, looking for instruments that had withstood the blaze, but with little success.

Wreckage of the mill (left); remains of musical instruments (right)

The converted mill before the devastating fire (above) and after (below)

Nor was hapless James Dewhirst, the young manager, at the end of his misfortunes. He was known locally as a daredevil motorcyclist and war hero who had been awarded the Croix du Guerre medal for his bravery in the Great War. With his livelihood, like his ballroom, reduced to ashes, Dewhirst made the decision to emigrate to South Africa. His intention was to work as an airmail delivery man, drawing on his experience as an RAF pilot in the war. However, just months after emigrating, disaster struck: he and a passenger were involved in a fatal flying accident when their plane plummeted to the ground, with Dewhirst at the controls. The pilot was killed instantly at the age of just 35. His wife and child had been due to join him in South Africa that same month.

As for the pleasure grounds at Goit Stock, their end, too, was in sight. A new ballroom was built but things were never the same, and the area was finally auctioned off in 1932 to a Mr Emmott. He bought the 90-acre estate for £2700, intending to strip the woods for timber and set up a building development. Luckily this plan never went ahead, and I wonder how many of those who enjoy serene woodland strolls at Goit Stock today know how very close they came to losing their solitary paradise in favour of a grim housing development or industrial estate.

A later plan to open a country club on the site also came to nothing, and thankfully West Yorkshire's Xanadu is now, as it was in the poet John Nicholson's time, a peaceful place where "meditation [may] rest reclin'd, lull'd by the neighbouring cataract's roar".

SITUATION.

Goit Stock is situated in the Harden Valley, between Harden and Cullingworth. **Cullingworth Station** is 20 mins. walk. **Trams to Allerton**, thence by Chara. via Wilsden, or **Trams to Bingley**, thence by chara. There is an half hour service of charas to and from Bingley, making the last return trip at **10-30 p.m.** Special Railway rates on application.

ADMITTANCE :

ADULTS   6d. Including Tax.
CHILDREN 3d.   "   "
SPECIAL TERMS FOR LARGE PARTIES.

Sky so blue it makes you wonder, if its heaven
    shining through ;
Earth so smiling way out yonder, Sun so bright
    it dazzles you ;
Birds a-singing, flowers a-flinging, all their
    fragrance on the breeze ;
Dancing shadows, green still meadows—
Dont you mope, you've still got these,

—— AT ——
GOIT STOCK WOODS.

ANNUAL FEATURES.

Easter Monday-

Easter Tuesday-

1st Saturday in May- CARNIVAL.
    Crowning of the May Queen of
    Harden. Dancing the Minuet
    by School Children.

Whit-Monday-

Whit-Tuesday-

1st Saturday in June

1st Saturday in July. MUSICAL FESTIVAL

August Bank Holiday-

Bowling Tide Week-ATHLETIC MEETING
    Adults and Juveniles
        CARNIVAL.

1st Saturday in September-

Last Saturday in September-
    Grand Firework Display.

A typical Goit Stock programme

*Motor cars and charabancs parked opposite the Malt Shovel pub
as their occupants enjoy a day out at Goit Stock (early 1920s)*

The Curious Case of the Cottingley Fairies

Did Sherlock Holmes creator Arthur Conan Doyle really believe in fairies – or was his well-publicised support for the faked Cottingley photographs simply a ruse to convert more people to spiritualism?

. . . .

IT'S now more than 30 years since pensioner Elsie Wright announced the unhappily ever after to a national fairytale, finally confessing fairy photographs she had taken with her cousin Frances Griffiths 66 years earlier were a hoax.

Elsie and Frances took the first two photographs by Cottingley beck in 1917, with a further three following in 1920. At the time many believed the images showed real fairies, and it wasn't until 1983 that the cousins publicly admitted they were fakes.

In the era of Photoshop it's hard to believe Elsie's fairy cutouts, copied from a book and propped up with hatpins, could ever have been taken for the genuine article. But by far the greatest mystery is how they fooled the father of detective fiction himself: Sherlock Holmes creator Arthur Conan Doyle.

After using the photos to illustrate an article in 1920, Doyle became their most vocal supporter. Critics dismissed him as a credulous old fool – but could he have had a hidden agenda?

When the photographs first came to light, Doyle was a man

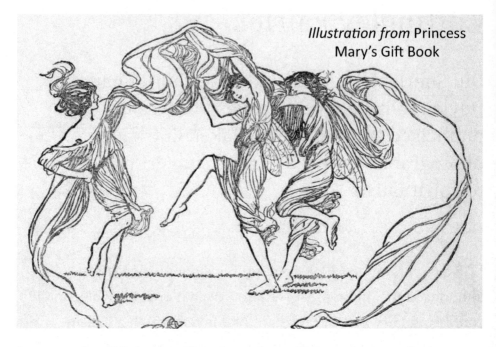

Illustration from Princess Mary's Gift Book

in mourning. He had suffered a string of bereavements, losing his son in 1918, followed in quick succession by his brother, two nephews and two brothers-in-law. The weight of grief drove Doyle into the arms of spiritualism, a belief system based around communication with the dead. He wasn't the only one: spiritualist beliefs surged following the First World War, as people struggled to cope with loss on an unprecedented scale.

Nevertheless, it seemed incredible that this educated man of science should suddenly profess belief in fairies. A doctor who had studied under forensics pioneer Dr Joseph Bell (the inspiration for Sherlock Holmes), Doyle was the creator of the most coolly logical mind in fiction – yet some of the clues he missed in "The Case of the Cottingley Fairies" would have made Holmes wince.

Frances and the Fairy Ring, 1917. The first photo taken, it brought the two girls to the attention of Sir Arthur Conan Doyle (© National Media Museum / Science & Society Picture Library)

Every suggestion that the photos might have been faked was summarily dismissed by Doyle. Even Elsie Wright's father, never convinced by the images, couldn't understand how the novelist had been duped "by our Elsie, and her at the bottom of the class".

One critic notes, for example, that the fairies appear two-dimensional, with different lighting to the girls. Ectoplasm, claims Doyle, is the explanation: it "has a faint luminosity of its own, which would largely modify shadows".

Similarly dismissed is the dimple on the gnome in the second photo, made by a pin mounted behind the card figure. This must be a belly button, enthuses Doyle – exciting evidence that fairy folk reproduce just as we do!

Elsie later confessed her figures were copied from a 1914 collection of children's stories, *Princess Mary's Gift Book*. One story included in the book is "Bimbashi Joyce" – by none other than Arthur Conan Doyle! The author would certainly have had a publisher's copy in his library: a clue his consulting detective surely wouldn't have missed.

Other evidence, such as the strangely-positioned limbs of the leaping fairy in the fourth photograph, is simply ignored (drawn freehand by Elsie, the figure clearly has one leg misaligned with its torso). Doyle also fails to explain the figures' suspiciously up-to-date "Parisienne" hairstyles (and what greater clue that the fairies were the work of a fashion-conscious teenager than that the in-vogue tresses of 1917 had evolved into flapper bobs by the time the second batch of photos was taken in 1920?).

Then there is the "clairvoyant" Geoffrey Hodson, sent by Doyle to Cottingley to corroborate the girls' stories. Hodson claimed to see lifeforms everywhere and made voluminous notes (in which an unlikely number of fairies are described as beautiful nude blondes gazing seductively at him). Elsie and Frances thought him a phoney and mischievously played along. Doyle, however, accepted all observations at face value.

"When you have eliminated the impossible, whatever remains, however improbable, must be the truth," Holmes famously said – but in this case Doyle was far too quick to eliminate the perfectly possible. He even hit on the exact method used to fake the images, before quickly dismissing it as too far-fetched: "Elsie could only have done it by cut-out images, which must have been of exquisite beauty, of many different models, fashioned and kept without the knowledge of her parents, and capable of giving the impression of motion when carefully examined by an expert. Surely this is a large order!"

At the time, the writer was on a crusade to open minds to the paranormal. "Anything which extends man's mental horizon… must have a good effect in breaking down materialism and leading human thought to a broader and more spiritual level," he wrote to spiritualist Edward Gardner. "When our fairies are admitted, other psychic phenomena will find a more ready acceptance."

Could Doyle have feigned belief to give the photos credibility and promote spiritualism? Frances Griffiths suspected so. In her memoirs, she suggests she became suspicious when Doyle offered to send Elsie to Ireland. The girls always claimed both of them were needed to summon fairies: why would Doyle ask Elsie to take photographs without her cousin, unless he knew it was she who produced the cutouts? And why didn't he go ahead with a planned visit to Cottingley to question the girls himself – could he have feared he would be proved wrong?

On the other hand, scientific background notwithstanding, Doyle was in many ways predisposed to believe in "little folk". His family were Irish, a country with a strong folklore tradition, and both his artist father and his uncle, celebrated *Punch* illustrator Dickie Doyle, were known for their paintings of elves and fairies. Members of Doyle's own family, including three of his children, claimed to have seen fairies. In his book *The Coming of Fairies,* he seems to write with genuine – even desperate – belief.

Whether or not Doyle truly had faith in the Cottingley fairies' existence, his endorsement elevated a schoolgirl prank to one of the most enduring hoaxes of the 20th century. And there is a further twist to the tale. Although she admitted faking the first four photographs, Frances Griffiths maintained to her death that she had seen fairies at the beck, and that the final photo, showing semi-transparent figures in a bower and declared "utterly unfakeable" by Doyle's photographic expert, was genuine. Was Sir Arthur right – could there, after all, be fairies at the bottom of the garden?

A painting of fairy folk by Arthur Conan Doyle's uncle, "Dickie" Doyle

WINDLESHAM
CROWBOROUGH

THE ATHENÆUM.
PALL MALL. S.W.I.

June 30

Dear Miss Elsie Wright

I have seen the wonderful pictures of the fairies which you and your cousin Frances have taken, and I have not been so interested for a long time. I will send you tomorrow one of my little books for I am sure you are not too old to enjoy adventures. I am going to Australia soon, but I only wish before I go that I could get to Bradford and have half-an-hours chat with you, for I should like to hear all about it. With best wishes

Yours sincerely

Mr Gardner told me about it.

Arthur Conan Doyle

Arthur Conan Doyle's letter to Elsie Wright

Photographing Fairies: A Timeline

1917: Irritated by adults who refused to believe there were fairies in the wood, 16-year-old Elsie Wright copied fairy illustrations from a book and used her father's camera to photograph them in front of her nine-year-old cousin, Frances Griffiths. The girls used the same method to capture Elsie with a gnome.

1919: The prank got out of hand when Elsie's mother, believing the photos to be genuine, showed them to the speaker at a lecture on fairy life. They attracted the notice of spiritualist Edward Gardner, who sent them to a photography expert for analysis. The expert reported that they were "genuine, unfaked photographs", single exposures, and showed "no trace whatsoever of studio work involving card or paper models". He also stated that the fairy figures had moved during exposure.

1920: The photographs came to the attention of Arthur Conan Doyle, who requested permission to use them in an article he was writing for *Strand* magazine.

Later that year, Gardner presented the girls with a camera apiece to take further photographs. This resulted in a second set of images, which Doyle used in a further article. Although some believed in the images, many critics felt that Doyle was the victim of an obvious prank, with one newspaper stating: "For the true explanation of these fairy photographs what is wanted is not a knowledge of occult phenomena but a knowledge of children."

1922: Doyle published a book about the Cottingley sightings, *The Coming of Fairies*. Afterwards the public gradually lost interest in the photographs, until the two girls involved were tracked down by reporters in the 1960s.

1983: Elsie and Frances gave several interviews in the 1960s and 70s, but only publicly admitted the photos had been faked in 1983. Although Elsie said all of the photographs were fake, Frances maintained the final image was genuine. She died three years later in 1986, followed by Elsie in 1988.

1997: A Hollywood film loosely based on the hoax, *Fairytale: A True Story*, was released.

1998: Two of the cameras used to take the photos, along with a signed copy of Arthur Conan Doyle's book *The Coming of Fairies* belonging to Elsie Wright, were donated to the National Media Museum in Bradford, where they are now on permanent display.

2009: Frances' daughter, Christine Lynch, appeared on *The Antiques Roadshow* with her mother's camera, handwritten memoirs and Gardner's original slides. They were valued at over £25,000.

Joseph Wright: From Donkey Boy to Oxford Don

Beginning work as a lowly donkey boy at the age of six, Joseph Wright was an unlettered Thackley millhand who could barely read a newspaper until he was 15. But life changed for the young man when he started work at Salts Mill in Saltaire. With access to the free schooling Sir Titus Salt provided for his workers, Wright eventually rose to become a world-leading linguist and Oxford don, counting Thomas Hardy, Virginia Woolf and JRR Tolkien among his friends and admirers.

. . . .

"THE details of Joseph's Wright's life read like a romance," wrote the Yorkshire dialect expert WJ Halliday. "But it is romance which is built on a solid foundation of character and indomitable will." It was this indomitable will that took Wright from an illiterate bobbin doffer for whom, in his own words, reading and writing were "as remote as any of the sciences" to a world-renowned linguist and Professor of Comparative Philology at the University of Oxford.

Joseph Wright was born into an impoverished Thackley family in 1855, the seventh son of a feckless father who earned his bread – when he was in work at all – as a cloth weaver and quarryman. The Wrights were so poor that they even spent a period in the workhouse at Clayton, and every family member capable of working was expected to start paying into the household pot as early as possible.

Little Joe was first put to work at age six as a quarry "donkey boy". Every day he would be expected to lead a donkey-drawn cart laden with tools to the local smithy for sharpening before returning them to the quarry. The ten-hour working day was long and gruelling for the little lad, and there was no time for schooling of any kind.

His fortunes improved at age seven when he was employed by Sir Titus Salt to work in his Saltaire mill as a bobbin doffer, removing the full bobbins from the spindles and replacing them with empty ones. Salt, the great paternalist, provided all his child workers with a free education at his factory school, and it was here that Wright first learned the basics of reading and writing. However, it was not until his early teens that Wright – now working as a woolsorter on what must have seemed a princely sum of £1 a week – began his studies in earnest. According to his biography, it was the outbreak of the Franco-Prussian war in 1870 that spurred the young man on, as he wished fervently that he could read a newspaper rather than receiving all the exciting accounts of battles second-hand from a more accomplished colleague.

Having taught himself to read, Wright found himself attracted to the study of languages and began studying the basics of Latin, German and French at Bradford Mechanics Institute's night school, in addition to maths and shorthand. So successful was he that at 18 he started his own night school in his mother's cottage, charging tuppence a week to attend. After managing to save £40 from his wages, Wright was able to pay for himself to attend the University of Heidelberg for a term before returning to Yorkshire to make his living as a teacher.

Rather brilliantly, Wright's hardworking mother Sarah, herself illiterate until the age of 45, also taught herself to read so she could share in the new world opened up to her son. Years later, when Wright took her to Oxford to show her his new home among the dreamy spires of academia, she is said to have remarked of All Souls College, "Eee, but it 'ud mek a grand Co-op!"

Attracted especially to the Germanic languages, Wright returned to Germany for six years in 1882 to pursue his studies and improve his knowledge of the language: it was here that he gained his PhD. A poor man still, he didn't have the luxury of being a full-time student: he earned his keep as a languages tutor teaching Old English and philology, as well as writing books and doing translations. While staying in Leipzig, he gained a reputation as a socialist firebrand, even being placed under arrest after making a speech in sympathy with striking workers.

After returning to England in 1888, Wright moved to Oxford, where he gave lectures at the university and continued to write and publish books on philology. Within just two years, he had so impressed the university's senior academics that a position was created especially for him – Lecturer in Teutonic Philology. Two years more and he had risen to the rank of deputy professor,

A 19-year-old Joseph Wright in his woolsorter overalls

eventually becoming a full professor in 1901. Five years before his death from pneumonia in 1930 age 74, he was given the prestigious appointment of emeritus professor.

Professor Wright put his success at the university down to pure graft. "Oxford is the most cosmopolitan city in the world," he once remarked. "A man can make his way at Oxford if he has the will; it does not depend upon birth or social status, but work."

Wright and his wife, a former student of his named Elizabeth Mary Lea whom he married in 1896, were hospitable people and often entertained at their home, named "Thackley" in deference to Wright's home town. The professor's Pavlovian party trick was to get the family pet, a Scottie called Jack, to lick his lips whenever he said the Gothic words for fig tree, *smakka bagms*.

Among his Oxford acquaintances was JRR Tolkien, who was a student and protégé of Wright's. It was the Yorkshire professor who encouraged young Tolkien to study Welsh, which would later have such a strong influence on his fiction. "Go in for Celtic, lad," Wright told him with typical frankness, "there's money in it." Tolkien's biographer notes that studying with the professor was one of the turning points of the young author's life.

Professor Wright was also a regular correspondent of the novelist Thomas Hardy and was greatly respected by Virginia Woolf, who wrote admiringly of his work in her diary.

But while hobnobbing with his illustrious friends, Dr Wright

Joseph Wright, Thackley, August 1928

had not forgotten his roots. With his humble Yorkshire origins and interest in languages, it is no surprise that he developed a fascination with regional dialects, and behind the scenes he was working on his magnum opus, the large and comprehensive *English Dialect Dictionary*. This was an enormous task, and as editor Wright spent years collating, cataloguing and cross-referencing material that in its raw form was said to weigh almost a tonne!

The work was eventually published by public subscription, with Wright composing over 3000 letters in a five-month period to secure the necessary funds. Part one of the *English Dialect Dictionary* finally became a published work on 1 July 1896, with five more volumes following. Dialect words from around the country were painstakingly recorded, with their variants, definitions and etymology, in a groundbreaking feat still unrivalled. Work on the dictionary also led to the formation of the Yorkshire Dialect Society, the world's oldest dialect society still in existence, in 1897.

"I am accustomed to get the very thing I want," Joseph Wright once told his wife. "When I once make up my mind that such a thing is the right thing to take place, I move almost heaven and earth to see that it *shall* take place." It was this Bradford boy's dedication, industry and that great Yorkshire characteristic, sheer stubborn bloody-mindedness, that made him who he was: a brilliant man and influential academic. The huge influence of his pioneering dialect dictionary in the field of linguistics cannot be understated.

To the Manor Born: The Bollings of Bolling Hall

What links the Native American princess Pocahontas, the "first female president of the United States", HG Wells's *The War of the Worlds* and the Bolling family of Bradford's Bolling Hall?

· ·

EDITH Wilson was the wife of President Woodrow Wilson. When a stroke left the president bedridden and partially paralysed in 1919, his First Lady assumed a leading role in affairs of state, controlling access to her husband and deciding which matters of policy were important enough to be brought to his attention. Because of the part she played in running the country from 1919 until Wilson left office in 1921, she's often referred to as "the secret president", as well as "the first female president of the United States".

Nancy Davis was a glamorous Hollywood film star who, in her MGM heyday, was romantically linked to stars including Peter Lawford and Clark Gable. She eventually married fellow actor Ronald Reagan in 1952, becoming First Lady in 1981 when he was inaugurated as the 40th president of the United States. Like Edith Wilson before her, Nancy Reagan exercised a powerful influence over her husband both personally and professionally. She was known for her work on drug awareness campaigns and as the originator of the "Just Say No" anti-drugs slogan.

George W. Bush, the second Bush to enter the White House (although according to some political commentators, probably not the last), divided opinion both at home and abroad as he steered the country through a challenging period that included the 9/11 terrorist attacks and the Iraq War. He also became famous for his frequent verbal gaffes, dubbed "Bushisms" ("I know the human being and fish can coexist peacefully...").

These three political heavyweights all played a part in the evolution of the United States political system, and all belong to American royalty: those wealthy, influential families that have been at the forefront of US social and political life for centuries. But they have something else in common: a blood tie. Each of them can trace their ancestry through a direct line back to one of Bradford's most significant families, the Bollings of Bolling Hall.

The oldest known reference to the manor of Bolling is in the Domesday Book, where "Bollinc" is recorded as the property of an individual named Sindi. Following the Norman conquest, it

Bolling Hall in West Bowling, now a museum (© Stuart Burrows)

passed into the possession – along with much of Yorkshire – of the king's crony Ilbert de Lacy, "the harrower of the North". "Ilbert has it [the manor] and it is waste," reads an account of the time.

However, by 1316 William de Bolling was listed as lord of the manor, and the estate remained in the family for several hundred years afterwards. The powerful Bollings also acquired land in Thornton, Allerton, Denholme, Wilsden, Hainworth, Horton, Clayton, Ilkley and Chellow.

A shaky period for the family in the 15th century saw them temporarily landless, with Robert Bolling and his ten children evicted from the ancestral home. Under the banner of Lord Clifford of Skipton Castle, Robert had espoused the Lancastrian cause in the ongoing War of the Roses and taken part in the Battle of Towton in 1461 – a vicious bloodbath that saw around 28,000 men slaughtered on the field of battle. The Yorkists were victorious, and the newly crowned King Edward IV hauled Robert up before Parliament on a charge of high treason. Bolling was fortunate enough to escape with his life, but he was stripped of his lands and wealth.

Robert was ultimately pardoned after the intercession of his ally and the king's brother, Richard, Duke of Gloucester – better known to history as much maligned hunchback Richard III. Regicidal Richard allegedly went on to murder Edward's rightful heirs, the "princes in the tower", and seize the throne for himself. However, he lost the crown for the Yorkists once and for all at the Battle of Bosworth Field in 1485, succeeded by a victorious Henry Tudor.

60

After living in straitened circumstances for a period of some 14 years, Robert Bolling's lands were eventually restored to him and his line in 1475 – in fact, Gloucester's endorsement seemed to hold such weight with the king that Bolling's wealth was actually increased.

The next Bolling of note is Robert's son Raynbron, a shady Sheriff of Nottingham-type figure who was employed as the king's bailiff in the reign of Henry VII. He was accused of exploiting his position by a large number of Bowling residents, stealing livestock for the Royal treasury through dirty tricks such as shearing sheep so their owners couldn't identify them and hiding cattle away for days before claiming them for the crown as waifs and strays. He was particularly hard on any toll dodgers who avoided the public highway, sending his men to beat them up and then rob them of many times the toll fee in recompense. Henry VII, who was trying to replenish the country's coffers after a long period of civil war, was known to turn a blind eye to dishonest practices by his bailiffs.

The estate at Bolling Hall left the paternal line when it was bequeathed by Raynbron's brother Tristram to his married daughter, Rosamund Tempest, in 1502. To his son by a second wife, Edward Bolling, Tristram left an estate in the hamlet of Chellow near Heaton, on the site of what is now the Bradford West Golf Course.

The Tempest family continued to occupy Bolling Hall until the end of the English Civil War – the period when the infamous Bolling Hall Ghost first appeared.

"Pity Poor Bradford" – the Bolling Hall Ghost

As one of Bradford's oldest buildings, it's no surprise that Bolling Hall is also reputed to be one of its most haunted, with rumours of mysteriously rocking cradles, glowing figures appearing in visitors' photographs and strange nocturnal disturbances. A reward of £50 was even offered by a local paper some decades back to anyone who dared spend the night there. No one took them up on the offer.

The most famous Bolling apparition appeared during the civil war in 1643: the ghost that supposedly saved Bradford. The legend goes that William Cavendish, Earl of Newcastle, was staying in the manor, which had been confiscated from the Parliamentarian Tempests to serve as a Royalist stronghold. Bradford was under siege and the earl had vowed that he would end the stalemate the very next day by putting every man, woman and child in the town to the sword. However, the earl had an overnight change of heart when he was visited by a ghastly female figure dressed all in white, who appeared to him wringing her hands and begging him to "pity poor Bradford". The following morning he revoked the order and told his men to kill only those who resisted them: just ten ultimately lost their lives.

At some point a branch of the Chellow Bollings relocated to London, where another Robert Bolling – known as "Robert the Immigrant" – was born in 1646. Robert was just 13 years old when he set sail for the New World in 1660, waving goodbye to England and her new king Charles II. His reasons for leaving are unknown, but it may be that just as the civil war had cost their Cromwell-sympathising Tempest cousins their home, the Restoration of the monarchy for some reason cost the Bolling family their country.

At any rate, Robert never returned to Britain after 1660, becoming the patriarch of a long line of American Bollings that continues to this day.

He landed in Virginia, where he eventually became a wealthy planter. It was here that, at 21, he met and married Jane Rolfe, the granddaughter of Pocahontas and her English husband John Rolfe (see p66). Sadly, Jane died giving birth to their only child, John, just two years later.

Robert Bolling, "The Immigrant"

Robert went on to have nine more children with his second wife, Anne Stith. In genealogical circles, descendants of Robert and Jane – such as Nancy Reagan and Edith Wilson – are traditionally known as the "red" Bollings. Descendants of Robert and Anne, such as the Bush family, are referred to as the "white" Bollings.

Over the years, the Virginia Bollings have shown a certain fascination with their Yorkshire heritage. Robert's son John even paid a visit to the county, where a surprised local remarked that he could speak English almost as well as herself. "Faith, madam, and I hope better," replied John, "or I would not talk it at all!"

Another descendant named Robert, born in 1738, was educated in Wakefield by a noted Yorkshire scholar and went on to become a prolific poet. He called his plantation in Buckingham County, Virginia, "Chellowe" after the Bradford hamlet where Edward Bolling once had his estate. And William Bolling, four generations removed from Robert "the Immigrant" and notable as the founder of the first US school for the deaf in the early 1800s, named his home in Goochland County, Virginia, "Bolling Hall".

Today, there is a Bolling Family Association in the US with a thriving community both online and offline – their website can be accessed at www.bolling.net. In addition to the Reagans, Wilsons and Bushes, famous direct descendants include writer and fashion designer Pauline de Rothschild, US senator John McCain and astronomer Percival Lowell, whose theory that what appeared to be canals on Mars were an artefact of an ancient civilisation – although of course later disproved – was a major influence on HG Wells's *The War of the Worlds*.

With presidents, First Ladies and even invaders from outer space all owing a debt to the Bollings, they could well now be dubbed "the Bradford family who went on to rule the world"!

Bolling Hall is now a museum and public library, boasting period furnished rooms that offer a fascinating journey through the lives of its previous occupants. Dare you go in the haunted Blue Room? The museum is free to visit and just a mile from Bradford City Centre. Opening hours are Wed–Fri 11am–4pm, Sat 10am–5pm and Sun 12noon–5pm.

Homes from home: Chellowe in Buckingham County, Virginia (top; © Amy Brailey), was built by the poet Robert Bolling in the 18th century, while Bolling Hall in Goochland County (bottom; © Virginia Department of Historic Resources) was William Bolling's 19th-century residence

Pocahontas and the Bollings

Matoaka, better known by her childhood nickname Pocahontas, was an indigenous American chieftain's daughter from the Virginia region. Famous in literature, song and of course Disney, she too has a connection with the Bradford Bollings. Many of the family's Virginian descendants can trace their ancestry back not only to the Bollings of Bolling Hall through Robert "the Immigrant", but to Pocahontas through Robert's first wife Jane Rolfe – her granddaughter.

According to an oft-told anecdote, at the age of 12 Pocahontas saved the life of an Englishman captured by her tribe, John Smith, by laying her head on a block where he was about to be executed. Impressed by the gesture, her father spared the captive's life.

Pocahontas was captured by the English in 1613. After marrying an Englishman, John Rolfe, she emigrated to Britain and became a feted celebrity, set up as the model of the 17th century's "noble savage" ideal and even being introduced to King James I.

In 1617, Pocahontas (who had taken the name Rebecca Rolfe following her baptism as a Christian), her husband and their young son Thomas boarded a ship to return to Virginia. However, just a short way into the journey Pocahontas became seriously ill. They returned to England, where she died at the age of just 22.

Although Pocahontas's story is often romanticised, historians now believe she was first and foremost a political strategist, working for peace between the native Virginians and English immigrants as well as seeking greater investment for the Jamestown settlement.

Her son Thomas grew up in England but returned to his mother's native Virginia as an adult, where he married and raised a family. His daughter Jane wed Robert Bolling in 1674.

A contemporary portrait of Pocahontas from 1616

The Keighley Poisoner

The trial of John Sagar, a Keighley workhouse master accused of poisoning his wife, shocked Victorian Yorkshire to its core. Scandal gripped the district as lurid details of the Sagars' life together emerged – sex, violence, adultery, illicit ménage a trois relationships and a string of suspicious infant deaths going back decades. Witnesses fell over each other to testify against the suspect and it seemed he was heading for the rope. But the trial collapsed, with Sagar walking from court a free man. An innocent scapegoat – or one of Yorkshire's most deplorable unpunished villains?

. . . .

WHEN blushing bride Barbara Scarborough wed her childhood sweetheart John Sagar at the age of 20, life seemed to stretch out before the young couple in a future full of hope and promise. But two decades later, the marriage ended abruptly in death, infamy – and the black shadow of the noose.

The events surrounding Barbara Sagar's death unfolded like the plot of a Penny Dreadful story: that favourite Victorian entertainment known for its sensationalism and gore. On the morning of 19th December 1857, the mistress of the Exley Head workhouse was found stark in her bed. She was discovered curled in the foetal position with fists clenched and tongue protruding from between her teeth, drenched in cold sweat and with an expression of agonising pain across her features. Less than a week before, Barbara had been fit and well, attending to her duties as usual. On Monday she had taken to her bed complaining of biliousness and a mild sore throat. The following Saturday, she was dead.

Tongues began to wag as town gossips shared ever more prurient stories of the Sagars' married life. Barbara's husband John had been seen "keeping company" with a workhouse guardian's daughter nearly 25 years his junior. He had tortured his wife both mentally and physically for years, even chaining her to the bed in a lunatic's bonds and, on one occasion, locking her in the "dead house" – the workhouse mortuary. Barbara had told friends and relatives that she believed her husband was trying to poison her, and that "if owt happened to me you might think it was murder". The Sagars' nine children had all died before the age of four – perhaps, it was whispered, at their father's hand.

It wasn't long before rumours of foul play reached the district coroner, Mr Thomas Brown, who felt the circumstances suspicious enough to halt the funeral plans and demand Mrs Sagar's body be

*The burial record for Barbara Sagar, signed by Haworth
curate Arthur Bell Nicholls (widower of Charlotte Brontë)*

submitted for an autopsy. When Barbara Sagar was finally committed to the soil of Haworth churchyard shortly before Christmas, she was missing her stomach, liver, kidneys and intestines.

The organs were sent to an eminent Leeds surgeon, George Morley, for analysis, and what he revealed at the subsequent coroner's inquest caused a sensation. Barbara Sagar's body had contained a significant amount of arsenic at the time of death – more than enough to kill. In addition, witnesses testified that all the symptoms of arsenic poisoning – frequent vomiting, an insatiable thirst, a burning sensation in the stomach and throat, a thick, white fur on the tongue – had been present in the week leading up to Mrs Sagar's death.

As if this wasn't suspicious enough, there was also Mrs Sagar's own testimony. She had frequently told friends and family that she believed her husband wanted to murder her, that her medicine had been poisoned and that it "burned her insides out". She asked several people to pray with her, stating that she was sure she would soon die. She also blamed medicine administered by her husband for the death of their last child, Samuel.

John Sagar, described as "a repulsive, dirty-looking man, about 45 years old and minus his left hand", with "forehead villainous low, and a square, repulsive countenance", had alone been responsible for preparing his wife's food and spooning out her medicine. He was known to have a history of cruelty towards her, told in more than words by the bruises found on her body during the autopsy. Witnesses claimed that at different times he had beaten his wife with a poker, threatened to break her legs, dragged her into the house by her hair, kicked her in the stomach, banged her head against a chest of drawers before leaving her unconscious for hours, locked her in the mortuary, and perhaps most degrading of all, chained her to the bed with an insane inmate's bonds in such a way that she could neither stand nor sit, but was forced into a crouching position for many hours.

And then there was the fact that John Sagar had previously worked as both a painter and a druggist, skilled in the procurement and use of arsenic. Yet despite strong grounds for suspicion, the coroner's jury ruled that "the deceased had died from the effects of poison – arsenic – but by whom administered they could not find".

The prisoner was proclaimed not guilty, and under normal circumstances would have been immediately released. But suspicion and public opinion were stacked so far against him that local magistrates took the affair into their own hands, and he was once again placed in Keighley lockup to await a further enquiry. If the evidence against him was found to be strong enough, he would be sent to York Assizes to face a criminal trial. A finding of guilt could mean only one outcome – death by hanging.

By the time of the magistrates' enquiry, weeks spent in the lockup had taken their toll on Sagar, who was "miserably dejected and broken in spirit". He refused his food and regularly cried out in his sleep, with police deeming it necessary to place him on suicide watch. Could his anguish have reflected fear for his life – or perhaps guilt over his devilish crimes?

The case caused a sensation in the town. Throngs of people – largely women – flocked to Keighley courtroom daily to witness the proceedings, with hundreds being turned away and police forced to use considerable violence to keep the crowds from riot. But excitement reached fever pitch on the third day of the enquiry, when 22-year-old Ann Bland took the stand.

The facts she disclosed of her relationship with the married couple were described as "too disgusting for publication" by the *Yorkshire Gazette* – other newspapers, however, were not so priggish, willingly lingering over every salacious detail. Ann testified that she had been the Sagars' joint lover for four years, coerced by Mrs Sagar into sharing the marital bed from the age of just 18. It was here, she said, that Mr Sagar had "taken her virtue". More shocking still, the couple had been in the habit of bedding other young women procured by Mrs Sagar – even, it was said, her own sister: a married woman named Martha Wadsworth.

Ann wasn't the only Bland to be publicly disgraced at the enquiry. Her father Thomas, one of the guardians responsible for the management of the workhouse, was censured for attempting to enter into improper correspondence with magistrate WB Ferrand. He was also seen trying to prevent his wife from giving evidence, and then refused to answer questions put to him on the stand. His behaviour led to strong words from the bench: "That you have committed the grossest perjury in the witness box is

Site of the Exley Head workhouse

clear to all here; and you leave it a disgraced man... it is clear that you are trying to screen this murder."

In fact it seemed as though a vast conspiracy to cover John Sagar's murderous inclinations was afoot. One workhouse resident, described as a "demented-looking woman", swore that the prisoner's sister Hannah Sagar had warned her not to testify, "not about bottles or anything". Martha Bland, mother of Ann, had intimated to friends that she knew Mrs Sagar had been poisoned, and that "there is plenty more which I know, but which I will never tell". A bottle labelled "julep", which Barbara Sagar had drunk from during her illness and which may have contained the poison that killed her, had conveniently disappeared.

It was enough for the magistrates. At the end of the enquiry, John Sagar was charged with the murder of his wife and committed to York Castle to await trial at the assizes. However, from day one of his court case things began to go horribly wrong for the prosecution.

First of all the judge ruled that the evidence of Ann Bland, which had caused such a sensation at the magistrates' enquiry, was inadmissible, since her relationship with John Sagar had taken place with the approbation of his wife. This was despite the considerable evidence that John Sagar and Ann Bland were having clandestine extramarital relations outside of their ménage without Barbara Sagar's knowledge – their adultery could well have been a motive for murder.

After pressure from Sagar's defence, it was also ruled that the prisoner's full history of cruelty to his wife could not be taken into account, a decision that provoked a public outcry.

However, the real stumbling block for the prosecution came when workhouse physician John Milligan, who had treated Mrs Sagar in her final week, gave a completely different testimony to the one he had given before magistrates. He had previously testified that he accepted the deceased had died from inflammation of the stomach caused by poison. However, to the York courtroom he stated that he did not believe the amount of poison found in the body could kill; that Mrs Sagar's death was entirely from natural causes. This directly contradicted the testimony of poisons expert George Morley, who had conducted the post mortem.

From that point the trial was dead in the water. The prosecution, knowing that no conviction could now be secured, withdrew their case, and John Sagar walked from court a free man.

The public were outraged. As far as they were concerned, a murderer who had tortured and ultimately killed his wife – and, it had been hinted in the press, may have dealt the same fate to at least some of his tiny children – had walked away unpunished. Judgement came down heavily on the man the public blamed for the collapse of the trial: the workhouse doctor John Milligan.

Milligan's reputation had not come well out of the affair.
At best he was seen as incompetent: a doctor who had failed to
spot the all-too-obvious telltale signs of arsenic poisoning in his
patient. At worst, he was viewed as an accomplice of the accused
who had deliberately screened his crimes and allowed him to
walk free.

In an attempt to salvage his professional reputation, Milligan
opened a bitter war of words in the *Leeds Intelligencer* with poisons
expert George Morley, but only ended up digging a deeper
hole for himself when Morley exposed Milligan's schoolboy
understanding of the chemical tests used to detect poison.
Nevertheless he kept his job, continuing as workhouse medical
officer for many years.

As for John Sagar, after the trial he returned to his previous
profession as a painter and lived out the remainder of his days
in Bradford. He married again in later life to a laundress named
Elizabeth, 22 years his junior, and eventually passed away
peacefully in his bed at the ripe old age of 71.

Was John Sagar a murderer? The clues are there to be seen.
His wife displayed all the symptoms of arsenic poisoning, and a
significant quantity of arsenic was found in her body after death.
Her food and medicine were administered almost exclusively by
her husband – a man with a long history of domestic violence and
adultery. She had stated on numerous occasions that her husband
was trying to kill her, and that her medicine had been poisoned.

A court of the time judged John Sagar an innocent man.
History may not be so kind.

Who Killed Barbara Sagar?

Clue 1: The Victim

Barbara Sagar had repeatedly stated that her husband was trying to kill her, that she was afraid she was being murdered, and that poison had been put into her medicine. She displayed most of the symptoms of arsenic poisoning in the last week of her life, and a considerable quantity of arsenic was discovered in her body after death.

Clue 2: The Suspect

John Sagar had worked as both a painter and a druggist, and would easily be able to procure arsenic. He had a long history of violence towards his wife, beating her with an iron poker when she angered him and chaining her to their bed.

Clue 3: The Mistress

Ann Bland was the Sagars' lover, sharing their marital bed – one of a number of young women procured by Mrs Sagar for her husband and herself. Witnesses testified that she had been seen "keeping company" with Mr Sagar, that he was in the habit of writing her love letters, and that their adultery could have provided a motive for murder.

Clue 4: The Children

All nine of the Sagars' children, born over a 20-year period, had died before the age of four. Gossip suggested their father may have had a hand in their deaths, and Mrs Sagar stated during her illness that Samuel, her last child, would have lived longer but for the medicine given him by her husband.

Clue 5: The Accessories

A number of people attracted public suspicion during the court case for their behaviour on the witness stand. Thomas Bland was accused by magistrates of withholding evidence, of perjury, and of trying to screen a murder. His wife was also accused of making "an exhibition" on the stand. Hannah Sagar, the prisoner's sister, was said to have warned off one of the workhouse paupers from giving evidence. And the institution's medical officer, John Milligan, repeatedly changed his evidence on whether or not Mrs Sagar had been poisoned, ultimately leading to the collapse of the trial.

Clue 6: The Missing Bottle

The prisoner John Sagar became anxious whenever bottles taken from the workhouse were produced in court, beating the dock and letting out melancholy moans. All were tested for arsenic, however, and nothing was found – with the exception of one bottle labelled "julep". Mrs Sagar had taken medicine from this bottle during her final illness, but despite numerous searches of the workhouse it was nowhere to be found.

Clue 7: The Stomach Pump

When the Sagars auctioned off the contents of their Cullingworth home in 1851 before taking up their positions at the workhouse – suspiciously setting no reserve despite a number of luxury items being included in the sale – one item listed was *a stomach pump*. Could this have been used during John Sagar's time as a publican on customers who didn't know when to say "when" – or could it have had a more sinister purpose in his chilling campaign of control against his wife and children?

A poster for the Sagars' 1851 auction of their household effects lists "1 stomach pump" among their property

The Moses of the West Riding

Bradford's John Wroe was a 19th-century cult leader and self-styled "prophet" whose rise to power was as sudden and dramatic as his later fall from grace. Short, ugly, illiterate and hunchbacked, Wroe was nevertheless a charismatic showman who wielded an influence that was anything but holy over his thousands of devoted followers. Some ended their days in the workhouse after contributing all their savings to fund his extravagant and debauched lifestyle. Still greater was the remorse of those who entrusted him with their daughters, in the notorious scandal of the seven virgins.

· ·

IN the winter of 1819, John Wroe of West Bowling lay dying. The fever from which he was suffering had reduced him to a mere skeleton, and his doctors instructed him to settle his affairs and prepare his soul for the next life.

Wroe's wife Mary sought in vain for a priest who would visit her afflicted husband and comfort him in his final hours, but in those days of soaring mortality rates human life was held cheap. Not one local minister was willing to leave his home for the sake of a poor Bradford woolcomber: an illiterate, bankrupt hunchback. Fearing it was now too late, Mary was forced to return home alone and administer what comfort she could by reading aloud from the Bible as her husband drew his final breaths.

But though he seemed on the brink of death, John Wroe made a full recovery that he would later claim was nothing short of miraculous. It left him a changed man. He began roaming the countryside with his Bible, sitting under hedges trying to make out passages of scripture and asking passers-by to help him with difficult sections (always a poor scholar, Wroe had left school barely able to read and write).

It was while wandering the fields in this way that Wroe experienced his first divine encounter. "I saw a vision with my eyes open; a woman came unto me who tossed me up and down in the field," he claimed. Wroe "struggled to get hold of her, but got hold of nothing" and knew she was a spirit.

This was the first in a series of fits, trances, visions and prophecies

Prophet John Wroe

that saw Wroe's fame spread rapidly during the 1820s. The time was ripe for a new religious leader to seize power. The cataclysmic events of the late 18th and early 19th centuries (which included the French Revolution and Napoleonic War), as well as drastic changes to working life, social structure and population size brought about by the ongoing Industrial Revolution, had given rise to an apocalyptic mood – many were convinced they were witnessing the end of days. In addition, the popular "prophetess" Joanna Southcott had died in 1814, leaving her followers rudderless and confused (Southcott had assured them she would live forever, so her death had come as something of a shock). Nothing could be easier than for a charismatic millenarian preacher like John Wroe, with a stock of Revelation quotes at his command and claims of a mandate from on high, to pick up where Southcott had left off. By 1822 he had been acknowledged as the leader of the Southcottian movement in the north of England, with followers numbering in their thousands.

Wroe's reported prophecies were a bizarre melding of the sublime and the ridiculous, the elaborate and the mundane. During one trance he was struck blind, and on recovering his sight he predicted that three years of plenty in the region would be followed by three years of scarcity. "As I have been six days blind, so would the nation be six years blind respecting the glorious time that was coming on," he predicted. "The first three years from that date would be plenty, but particularly the third year, for in Bradford, and at all other places, the best beef would be sold for 4d per pound; and all other things would be equally cheap." Perhaps critics might have wondered at the Almighty's sudden interest in the minutiae of Bradford grocery pricing, but Wroe's followers were to have the last laugh – the early 1820s were indeed prosperous, followed by a depression in the textile industry in 1823-25. On another occasion Wroe prophesied that a light would break forth from the spot on which he stood to enlighten the gentiles of Ashton-under-Lyne. Sure enough, this field later became the site of the Ashton gasworks...

Wroe's other predictions included ships without sails that could travel against the wind, horseless carriages and horseless ploughs. Some visions, however, were less prescient. Perhaps the most surreal was the command Wroe received in June 1827, that he must deliver prophecies at the marketplace in Bradford with his bare buttocks exposed – a command which he dutifully obeyed, no doubt to the great surprise and amusement of local shoppers. Another bizarre vision told him that he must go home and "destroy all pictures, portraits or likenesses of anything he had created or caused to grow, whether of iron, stone, wood, cloth or paper, and everything of a black colour that could be found within the house."

While to his acolytes Wroe was a powerful orator and prophet, to many of those outside the movement the little man riding about on his donkey preaching hellfire was a figure of fun. In Bradford he was nicknamed "Pudding" Wroe due to his customary answer on awaking from a trance and being asked what he could fancy to eat – "Nowt but pudding". One day, after being taunted with the nickname by all the urchins in the neighbourhood, Wroe

The Baptism of Prophet Wroe

In February 1824, at the height of his fame, 30,000 people gathered on the banks of the River Aire at Apperley Bridge (near Idle) to witness Wroe's public baptism. The crowd was treated to quite a spectacle as the prophet arrived on a donkey, wielding an iron rod and followed by a troupe of musicians. Wroe had predicted that on entering the freezing water, "glory-making sunbeams would illuminate his head", but the sky was cloudy and he was forced to linger on the bank in the hope that the weather would improve enough to fulfil his prophecy. However, many in the crowd had turned up in the hope of seeing a miracle, expecting that Wroe would either part the waters like Moses or walk on the surface like Christ, and when he appeared unwilling to approach the river they turned nasty. "He dussn't go in! He's running away!" some shouted, followed by cries of "Drown him! Drown him!" Wroe was forced to beat a hasty retreat as the now riotous crowd pelted him and his followers with mud and stones.

returned to his wife and family in a foul mood. On asking what was for dinner, he received the reply from the children, "Nowt but pudding!", which drove him into a rage. Turning to his wife, he said, "I'll tell thee what, lass, I wi'nt have yon stuff called 'pudding' ony more." "Why, lad! What are t' bairns to call it, then?" she answered. "They mun call it, 'soft meat'!" came the reply.

The religious movement Wroe founded, which he named the Society of Christian Israelites, chose the unprepossessing Lancashire mill town of Ashton-under-Lyne for its headquarters.

This town, they believed, would be the New Jerusalem foretold in the Book of Revelation, the dwelling place of God's chosen people following the imminent apocalypse. The Christian Israelites were easily identifiable on the streets of Ashton, dressed in their long, white robes and with the men each wearing a full beard. Beards were uncommon, even comical, before the mid-19th century, and the sect members were nicknamed "beardies" by mocking locals.

A blue plaque in Ashton-under-Lyne, outside the Odd Whim pub – this was originally one of four gatehouses built by Wroe to surround his New Jerusalem

The "beardies" were instructed to follow strict Mosaic law: only kosher meat was to be eaten, snuff, tobacco and alcohol must be given up, and circumcision was mandatory for all male members. Wroe set the example by undergoing a public circumcision in April 1824. However, later the same year the group attracted criticism after an infant died following a botched operation. The surgeon, Henry Lees, was put on trial for manslaughter but was ultimately cleared due to inconclusive medical evidence. Nevertheless, much damage had been done to the public image of the hitherto harmless-seeming cult, who were dubbed "pseudo-Semitic cranks" by one newspaper.

Women, too, were expected to follow the law of Moses to the letter, particularly when it came to their sexual behaviour. Those found to be unchaste were made to sit through a fierce sermon delivered by Wroe before being taken to a "cleansing room", where they were stripped naked and beaten with a birch rod. This flagellation rite cropped up again during the "seven virgins" trial of 1830, when one of the young women involved alleged that Wroe had coerced her into inflicting the same "purifying" punishment on him.

Wroe's followers may have been convinced of his claims to divine inspiration, but even at the height of his popularity there were plenty of others willing to denounce him as a charlatan. One man, a neighbour of Wroe's in Bradford, claimed that he had observed the prophet through a window when he was supposed to be in one of his holy trances, tucking into a plateful of beefsteak, pickled cabbage and oatcake. A similar incident occurred when Wroe, who was supposedly doing penance in the fields of Pudsey and living only on nuts and berries, was found eating a meal of mutton, new potatoes and wine brought by his wife from a nearby pub. Caught in the act, an angry mob punished him for his deceit by dragging him through the streets and repeatedly ducking him in a horse-pond. On another occasion Wroe claimed he needed £80 for a religious mission, and the sum was swiftly raised from among his congregation. Wroe took the money and departed on his "mission": however, he was found some time later drinking hot whisky and water with two prostitutes in a Manchester pub.

The prophet was dogged by sex scandals from as far back as 1823, when he was found to have got one of his female followers pregnant. In an attempt to appease her angry relations, Wroe announced that the woman would give birth to Shiloh, the second messiah whose birth would herald the coming apocalypse. Much preparation was done in anticipation of Shiloh's birth – but to Wroe's humiliation, when the baby was born it was a girl. This child was considered to be in so much danger that her identity was kept secret for 150 years. Only in the 1970s was her name finally released – Sarah Hague, a respected lifelong spinster of Ashton, who died in 1907 at the age of 83.

A few years later, Wroe was hit by another scandal when he was accused of molesting a young servant girl at his farmhouse in Tong. The alleged victim was an apprentice woolcomber aged just 13, who claimed she was pregnant by Wroe. A warrant for his arrest was issued, but although it was found that he had misused and ill-treated her, the girl did not give birth and the rape charge wasn't pursued.

The best-known scandal involving Wroe, however, is the infamous case of the seven virgins, which has inspired both a novel and a BBC television drama. In 1830 Wroe announced that he had received a command from the Lord: the congregation must provide him with seven virgins, "proved to be so by strict examination", to "wait upon, nourish and comfort him, and be as wives unto him, except that he should not carnally know them". They were supposed to live with Wroe "in a state of innocence, and thus display a pattern of purity to the whole people". He was to protect them from the world and its impurities, "and as he overcame the lust of the flesh, so would the whole new house of Israel overcome." A number of Christian Israelite families duly gave up their daughters to Wroe, but after travelling with him on his missions for several months, three of the girls – one only 15 years old – disclosed shocking details of their lives with the prophet, alleging lying, sexual misconduct and seduction.

Wroe was placed on trial by church elders, where many salacious details of his behaviour came to light. According to a newspaper report, Wroe had coerced one of the girls into "the most revolting and unnatural act of indecency which can be conceived, with the mention of which we will not defile our columns", and there were further allegations "too gross to be mentioned". While the judge at his trial ultimately refused to condemn Wroe for his "lax morals", comparing himself to Pontius Pilate washing his hands of Christ's blood, anger against the prophet was great in both Ashton and Bradford, and he was forced to flee to Wakefield to escape rioting.

The Christian Israelite Society never fully recovered from the negative publicity generated by this case, which also spelled the end of Wroe's authority in Ashton-under-Lyne. Christian Israelites in the town declined from as many as 500 in their heyday to only 150 by the time of the 1851 census.

Even after the scandal, however, Wroe seems to have had no trouble scamming money from his remaining devotees. In 1854 he claimed he had been commanded by the Lord to build a home for the long-expected Shiloh. His followers were asked to contribute

A Christian Israelite church in Sydney, Australia

as much as they could, no less than 10% of all they had regardless of income, and it was said that some ended life in the workhouse after giving up all their savings to the project. £2000 – a vast sum at that time – was raised to build an opulent mansion in Wrenthorpe, near Wakefield: Melbourne House. Incredibly, Wroe managed to have the land for Melbourne House (plus a 100-acre farm surrounding it) bought in his own name, seemingly with no questions asked. Although he drew up a will leaving everything to the society in the presence of the Church elders, two weeks later he privately amended the document to leave everything to his children and grandchildren, having successfully conned his followers into footing the bill for what was essentially a private residence. The house remained in the Wroe family for several generations and exists today as an office building.

Two years later, Wroe was in need of money again and declared that the Lord had commanded him to have gold rings made for every member of the society – these would be used to identify the chosen people on the day of judgement. He demanded £1 3s 6d from every member to supply the rings: however, when one wary Israelite thought to test his in nitric acid, it was discovered to be not of gold at all but a base metal and worth barely two shillings.

But neither financial scams nor sex scandals, Yorkshire puds nor bare buttocks, were enough to sink Prophet John Wroe, and he maintained a small but loyal following until the end of his life. While the Christian Israelite Society waned in Britain, it continued in America, Poland and Australia – indeed, it continues in these places to this day.

It was while visiting the Church at Fitzroy, Australia, in 1863 that the Yorkshire Moses finally met his maker. The 81-year-old had been collecting subscription money from members there and seemed in good health when he died suddenly – much to the anger of Christian Israelites in the area, who immediately demanded their money back as like Joanna Southcott before him, John Wroe had promised them he would never die. Such was his loyal followers' faith in him, however, that for many years after his death a room was kept at Melbourne House with his slippers warming by the fire – just in case he should return as the promised Shiloh.

The Hangman Cometh...

James Berry, the son of a Bradford wool-stapler, held many jobs during his life: beat bobby, boot salesman, pig farmer and even preacher. But it was his gruesome role as Britain's foremost hangman that earned him the respect and fear of the Victorian underworld – not to mention his own waxwork in Madame Tussaud's "Chamber of Horrors". Berry despatched over 130 condemned prisoners during his time as public executioner: he even believed he had hanged Jack the Ripper himself. Yet in later life Berry became an ardent and vocal capital punishment abolitionist, touring the country lecturing on the ineffectiveness of the death penalty.

· ·

"COMPETITIVE salary and travel opportunities available for right candidate. Must be willing to work unsociable hours. Strong stomach essential."

So might a job advert have read for one of Victorian England's most unpopular jobs, the man tasked with delivering the ultimate punishment: the state executioner. It's hard now to imagine what might have tempted someone to apply for such a role, other than sadism or morbid fascination. But for 32-year-old James Berry, a Bradford boot salesman and retired policeman, the reasons were

simple: justice, divine command –
and the money.

Berry, the 13th of 18 children
born to a well-to-do Heckmondwike
wool-stapler, had left the Bradford
police force in 1882 after serving
for eight years, feeling he had been
unfairly passed over for promotion
to detective, and was struggling
to support his wife and growing
family. An executioner could earn
good money – up to £350 a year
at a fee of £10 per hanging, Berry

James Berry

calculated – and his acquaintance with the previous hangman,
William Marwood, had convinced him he could build upon
existing methods to provide a humane and instantaneous
death for the condemned. Although he found the idea of
performing executions distasteful, he didn't feel it was in any
way dishonourable or immoral – Berry believed that the words
of Genesis 9:6, "whoso sheddeth man's blood, by man shall his
blood be shed", were a divine dictum which a Christian society
had a duty to uphold. His experience as a policeman had also
taught him that capital and corporal punishment (in the form of
whippings – "the cat") were the only effective legal deterrents for
those he classed as career criminals. When the position of public
executioner became vacant following his friend Marwood's death
in 1883, Berry leapt at the opportunity.

Newgate Gaol, where many of Berry's hangings took place

He wasn't the only one. 1400 applicants sent their credentials to the Home Office after Marwood's death, begging to be considered for the job. What could have motivated so many people to apply for a role that would have made them a social pariah (as Berry was to discover) can only be imagined. However, the applicants were whittled down to a shortlist of just 20.

Berry's name made the list, but the appointment was eventually given to a Dewsbury man, Bartholemew Binns – largely, Berry felt, because of a campaign against him by his own relatives, who wrote to the Home Office begging them not to sully the name of a respectable family by granting Berry the appointment. This only made him more determined to obtain the role if it ever became vacant again, and he began in-depth research into the science and practice of execution.

He did not have to wait long for a chance to reapply. The incompetent Binns, who became known as "Britain's worst hangman", held the position for less than four months before he was sacked for drinking on the job and a series of botched executions.

By the time the role became vacant again, Berry had already performed one double hanging after offering his services to magistrates in Edinburgh, who wanted a man to execute a couple of miners found guilty of murdering two gamekeepers while out poaching. After giving the young men the only thing that could now benefit them – a quick and painless death – Berry received glowing references from the prison doctors, governor and magistrates. When he applied to fill Binns's shoes in March 1884, he was accepted without competition.

At that time, hangmen received no formal training and were expected to provide all their own equipment. The Home Office saw them very much as blunt instruments of the state: they had little interest in how or why the executioners did their jobs, as long as they were discreet and the outcome for condemned prisoners was a clean and uneventful death that wouldn't outrage "public decency". Berry's previous connection with Marwood, who had coached his protégé in his methods, was helpful to him in gaining the appointment, as was the fact that he already had all his own equipment – some hanging ropes he had bought from Marwood, along with leather leg and wrist pinioning straps he had had made.

In his time as executioner, Marwood pioneered what became known as the "long drop" method. In the early days of public hangings there had been no drop at all: prisoners were simply

noosed and then hoisted up by the executioner, suspended above
ground as they suffered a slow, painful death by strangulation.
By the time Marwood took the position, the short drop method
was in use: a trapdoor opened and the prisoner fell a distance of
around three feet. For some, death was instantaneous: however,
for most, strangulation was still the cause of death. This suited
Victorian society just fine: strangulation may have been slow and
painful, but it was clean and left a body which was both whole
and virtually unmarked; unlike, say, beheading by guillotine –
less painful, but far more gory.

Marwood theorised that he could cater to the over-nice,
somewhat hypocritical sensibilities of the age while still ensuring
a quick and humane death for prisoners, and after practising
on cement blocks of different weights, he created the long drop.
Using this method, the length of drop was calculated according
to the size and weight of the prisoner. If the drop was estimated
accurately, the spinal cord would be dislocated and death would
be instant.

Berry inherited Marwood's table of drop calculations, as well
as his commitment to humanely despatching those destined to
die at the executioner's hands. He spent some time fine-tuning
Marwood's calculations to take into account factors such as neck
muscle development, practising by hanging weighted sacks at his
home in Bradford and exhibiting a calm, scientific detachment
that seemed almost at odds with his commitment to merciful
execution. But despite all his research, less than two years into the
job Berry's use of the long drop led to a traumatic hanging that

caused him to drastically revise his calculations – and haunted his nightmares for many years to come.

Robert Goodale, a market gardener from Norwich, had been sentenced to hang for the murder of his wife Bathsheba in September 1885: after an argument, he had knocked her unconscious with an axe handle before drowning her in a well. Berry was to carry out the execution. There had been great public interest in what had been dubbed "The Walsoken Tragedy", and on the morning Goodale's sentence was to be carried out, a number of newspaper men had gathered alongside prison staff to witness the event.

Goodale was a large, corpulent man weighing over 15 stone, and Berry had decided to shorten the usual drop for a man of his height and weight by two feet to account for the prisoner's lack of muscle development. But it wasn't enough.

The day of Goodale's execution was a shambles from start to finish. The prisoner was, understandably, terrified of the noose and fought his captors all the way. Berry and the warders had to call in outside help to pinion the man's arms behind his back, and then virtually dragged him to the scaffold. On catching sight of the gallows, Goodale instantly fainted, and the warder who held him upright very nearly tumbled through the trapdoor with his prisoner when Berry pulled the lever to send Goodale to his fate.

It was then that witnesses saw the rope go slack. Berry thought the noose must have slipped off and cautiously approached the trapdoor, dreading to see the man injured or dead at the bottom of the drop. But the truth was immeasurably more horrible.

Goodale's body was there at the bottom of the drop – and so was his severed head. The drop had been too long for the stout man, and he had been completely decapitated.

The newspaper reporters present did their job, writing up the incident as "The Goodale Mess". The condemned man would have died instantly, unlike the three people who, during Berry's time as executioner, are known to have suffered strangulation after a drop that was too short. Yet the sight of the man's body awash with blood, his head beside him, had a profound effect on the hangman. He was cleared at an inquest of any wrongdoing, but Berry was determined that he would never again be responsible for ending someone's life in such a gruesome and traumatic manner. He stepped up his research, creating a new, more scientific table of drops, and thanks to Berry's refinement of the long drop method, Robert Goodale is notable as the last man to die from decapitation in the British justice system.

The hangman's status in Victorian society was an odd mix of contradictions. While the public were largely in support of capital punishment, the man who actually did the state's dirty work was nevertheless regarded with a mixture of horror and fascination by his fellow creatures. James Berry was propelled to celebrity status when he took on the role, even being given his own waxwork in Madame Tussaud's, yet it was also an isolating experience. He was even forced to buy his home and the six neighbouring houses in Bilton Place, Bradford (off City Road) because he found landlords resented the way that letting to a public hangman drove away other tenants.

| QUOTE | | *Bradford,* ....*189* |
| No. .... | | YORKS. |

Sir,

I beg leave to state in reply to your letter

of the .... *that I*

am prepared to undertake the execution you name of

....

at .... *on the* ....

I also beg leave to state that my terms are as

follows : £*10 for the execution,* £*5 if the condemned*

is reprieved, together with all travelling expenses.

Awaiting your reply,

I am, Sir,

Your obedient Servant,

James Berry.

The High Sheriff,

for the County of ....

The form used by Berry stating his terms and fees

On one occasion, he successfully sued a newspaper for libel over some fabricated sensationalist stories they claimed Berry had confided in an interview, as well as a description of his appearance that suggested the hangman was little short of a psychopath:

> *He is a powerful, thick-set man, of about medium stature, and his countenance is not an unpleasant one at a first glance, though upon closer study one discovers that the face reveals the lack of several moral elements in the man's composition, which seems to indicate that the Creator designed him especially for the ends he serves... A phrenologist* would perhaps find that the cranial bumps that indicate sense and shame, pity and sympathy, are not particularly well developed upon the head of Mr. Berry.*

Berry writes with a sort of grim drollery about his experiences with the public in his 1892 memoir, *My Experiences as an Executioner*. At the start of his tenure as hangman, Berry had a set of business cards printed up which he would leave at the prisons he visited (although the Home Office kept a list of approved executioners, the hangman was effectively a freelancer hired on an ad hoc basis by the sheriff of each district, so a bit of self-promotion by Berry – while macabre – was in keeping with his position). He also seems to have enjoyed using these to discomfit members of the public who annoyed him. The following anecdote is typical of his experiences:

---

* Phrenology was a pseudo-science popular in 19th-century Britain, which suggested that skull shape could be used to predict personality traits

In 1887 when I had to go to Dorchester, to hang Henry William Young for the Poole murder, I stayed at Bournemouth, and took a room in a Temperance Hotel. During the evening I got into conversation with the landlady, who was much interested in the subject of executions, and who appeared to like to discuss it. She was decidedly "down on" Berry, " the hangsman," and expressed herself very freely as to his character and disposition; amongst other pleasant things, saying that he was a man without a soul, and not fit to have intercourse with respectable people. Of course, I smilingly agreed with everything that she had to say, and chuckled quietly to myself about a little surprise that I had in store for her. The surprise came off at bed-time, when she handed me my bedroom candle, and in return I handed her my card. The good lady nearly fainted.

During his time as executioner Berry was noted for his professionalism, but privately the trauma of his experiences on the scaffold had started to weigh heavily on him. Teetotal when he first took on the role, in later years it was Berry's usual habit to steady his nerves with a few drinks – and then perhaps a few more – after each hanging.

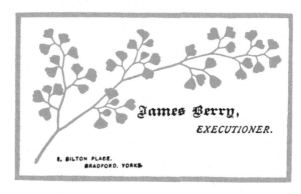

Berry's business card

Berry's Heirs: The Pierrepoint Dynasty

It's a curious fact that of five public executioners who served between 1884 and 1956, four were from the Bradford area. James Berry, of course, was the first. The other three were provided by the same Clayton family, the notorious Pierrepoints, whose "reign" as executioners totalled 55 years. All three Pierrepoints used the long drop method developed by Marwood and honed by Berry.

Henry Pierrepoint had dreamed of becoming an executioner like his hero Berry since the age of 12, when he had eagerly read about the exploits of Berry and his successor, James Billington, between shifts at the Clayton worsted mill where he worked. He repeatedly wrote to the Home Office to request the position, and in 1901, at the age of 23, he achieved his goal. Henry carried out 105 executions in nine years, including baby killers Amelia Sach and Annie Walters, and successfully persuaded his brother Thomas and son Albert to join the family business. However, his tenure ended when he turned up drunk to a job and fought with his assistant, a Rochdale hairdresser named John Ellis, who reported the incident to the Home Office.

His brother Thomas worked as a hangman for 37 years and is credited with 294 hangings. He was still performing executions when he was well into his seventies, eventually retiring in 1946. One of his most high-profile prisoners was the poisoner Frederick Seddon, an arrogant killer who murdered his trusting neighbour with arsenic in order to steal her savings.

Most famous of all is Henry's son Albert, landlord of the Help the Poor Struggler pub and part-time hangman. Unlike previous executioners, he became something of a national hero after terminating the lives of a number of Nazi war criminals following World War II. These included William Joyce, better known as

Lord Haw-Haw, and defector John Amery, whom he called "the bravest man I ever hanged". Like his father Henry, Albert had wanted to be a hangman from a young age, and it's believed he executed 433 men and 17 women during his career.

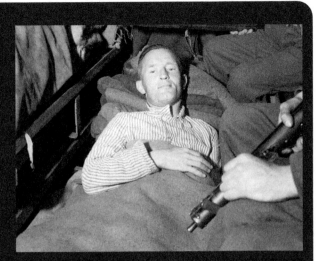

William Joyce, "Lord Haw-Haw"

One of his more traumatic executions was Ruth Ellis, the last woman to be hanged in England, who had murdered her lover in a crime of passion. Pierrepoint described Ellis, a mother to two young children at the time of her execution, as a courteous and cooperative prisoner.

Another upsetting incident occurred when Pierrepoint was called upon to hang a drinking buddy, James Corbitt, who had murdered his mistress after getting drunk in the hangman's pub.

Pierrepoint was known as Britain's most efficient hangman, and a macabre mythology grew up around him – for example, the fiction that he could tell a man's height, weight and the length of drop needed to execute him just by shaking his hand.

Like Berry, Pierrepoint eventually concluded that capital punishment was not an effective deterrent. "The fruit of my experience has this bitter after-taste," he wrote, "that I do not now believe that any of the hundreds of executions I carried out has in any way acted as a deterrent against future murder."

Berry never drank on the job, but his increasingly common practice of "holding court" in pubs after executions – discussing the hanging and distributing his business cards to fellow drinkers – was making him no friends at the Home Office, and questions were even asked in Parliament about his lack of discretion. Meanwhile, Berry was becoming increasingly preoccupied by the rights and wrongs of his calling. He couldn't help feeling that execution, which he still supported in theory, was not right in every case – that some of those he hanged had the capacity to reform and become valuable members of society. He was also starting to worry that not all of those who swore their innocence on the scaffold were lying, and that he was the instrument of a miscarriage of justice in some cases.

Berry's reign as executioner ended in 1891 following a disastrous hanging in which the condemned man was given a drop that was too long. He didn't lose his head like Goodale, but the blood vessels in his neck were ruptured in a partial decapitation.

Although Berry wasn't at fault – his recommended length of drop had been overruled by the prison doctor – he still came in for the lion's share of censure, both for the botched hanging and for the way he had conducted himself in angrily and vocally opposing the doctor who had overruled him. After being pilloried by the press and public, Berry wrote to the Home Office to ask them to remove his name from the list of official executioners. What he didn't know was that the Home Office had already made the decision to remove his name. Berry was attracting too much attention for their liking, and his lack of discretion had been noted.

Berry now feared that he would become unemployable. He managed to scrape a living for a few years afterwards by exploiting his celebrity, touring America and Britain and giving lectures on his kills. He took with him the "black museum" he had amassed during his years as an executioner: the rope from every hanging he had ever conducted, a collection of relics from the killers he had despatched, death warrants for all the prisoners, and magic lantern slides of their photographs. He could even make a few bob by letting members of the public pose with their favourite murderer's hanging noose around their neck while Berry pinioned their hands behind their back. But he was a hit-and-miss speaker and eventually this rather sick source of income dried up. He tried his hand at various careers after this, finally settling at Walnut Tree Farm on Bolton Road, Bradford, and setting up as a pig farmer, but with only moderate success.

His experiences at the gallows seemed to have left Berry with a form of post-traumatic stress disorder. In his living room he still kept photographs of every person he had hanged framed on the wall, and he was tortured by nightmares about their final moments. Like Albert Pierrepoint over 60 years later, he had now come to the conclusion that capital punishment was ineffective and unnecessary, and that it placed an unfair burden on the one man relied on by the public to carry out the ultimate sentence – the executioner (in his 1905 book *The Hangman's Thoughts Above the Gallows*, he writes that "the law of capital punishment falls with terrible weight upon the hangman and that to allow a man to follow such an occupation is doing him a deadly wrong"). He had also developed a superstitious belief that the "demons" of every murderer he had ever hanged had been absorbed by him at the point of death, and he would now be damned for their crimes as well as his own. Eventually, guilt over his past career caused him to become suicidal, and on 13 February 1904 he bought a one-way ticket from Midland Railway Station (now Bradford Forster Square), planning to end his life by leaping from the carriage into the path of another train.

As he sat at the station, sobbing and begging his deceased mother to comfort him, he was observed by a young man who was a member of the congregation at the Bowland Street Mission in Manningham, run by American preacher Smith Wrigglesworth. The young man comforted Berry and took him to the mission to be "saved", and from that day Berry became a devout Christian. The mission announced that "Mr Berry fully surrendered himself, accepted God's precious gift and was at once filled with rest and joy, praising God".

Berry spent the remainder of his life as an evangelist preacher. He toured the country giving sermons on the evils of capital punishment, which he now believed should be entirely abolished. Writing just before his death, he said, "my experiences have convinced me we shall never be a civilised nation while executions are carried out in prison."

James Berry passed away at his home, Walnut Tree Farm, on 21 October 1913. He was 61.

Berry's Rogues Gallery

James Berry executed over 130 convicted murderers in his eight years as public executioner. These were some of the most noteworthy.

John "Babbacombe" Lee, 1885

John Lee was a 19-year-old domestic servant who was convicted of killing his employer, an elderly former lady-in-waiting and friend of Queen Victoria. He was sentenced to death based on weak and circumstantial evidence, subsequently finding fame as "the man they couldn't hang". Berry refers to this incident in his memoirs as being one of two terrible experiences – the other being the decapitation of Robert Goodale the same year.

Three attempts were made to hang Lee, and on each attempt the trapdoor failed to open. Each time the prisoner was removed and the trapdoor tested, and each time it worked perfectly, but once the prisoner was again placed over the drop the trapdoor failed to open. Unsure what to do, the prison governor wrote to the Home Secretary, who made the decision to commute Lee's sentence to life imprisonment.

An official report into the incident blamed incorrect assembly of the gallows mechanism, but many put it down to divine providence – the evidence against Lee was weak and he wasn't meant to be hanged. When he was released after serving 20 years, Lee was able to live off his celebrity as "the man they couldn't hang" for the rest of his life.

Elizabeth Berry, 1887

Elizabeth Berry's crime was a particularly unpleasant one. Her victim had been her own daughter, a ten-year-old girl called Edith. The good-looking 31-year-old widow had poisoned the little girl with arsenic she had obtained through her job as a workhouse nurse, and although she was never tried for the crimes, she may have murdered her husband, son and mother in the same way. Her ostensible motive for murder was the £10 she would receive in life insurance when her daughter was dead, and the £12 a year she would save on her upkeep. One strange fact of the case was that although not related, James and Elizabeth Berry were acquaintances

Elizabeth Berry

– they had even danced together at a policeman's ball two years earlier. On the day of the execution, the prison governor joked with the executioner, "I didn't realise you were going to hang an old flame, Berry" – until that time, the hangman hadn't realised who she was. Berry stated later that he particularly hated having to hang women.

Israel Lipski, 1887

Israel Lipski was an umbrella salesman of Polish-Jewish descent convicted of murdering a pregnant young woman by forcing her to consume nitric acid. The behaviour of the press and public leading up to Lipski's execution disgusted Berry, who swore he would never again hang a Jew.

In Victorian London anti-Semitism was rife, and Lipski had been universally deplored both for his crime and his religion. On the day of his execution a mob of thousands gathered outside the prison, where according to Berry a number of Jewish people in the crowd "were kicked and cuffed about, and insulted in every imaginable manner; for the hatred displayed by the mob was extended from Lipski to his race". When the black flag was raised to signal that the execution had been successful and Lipski was dead, it was greeted by three cheers. This was in strong contrast, Berry observed, to the behaviour of the crowd at the next execution he presided at, that of a convicted child killer. The hangman was "struck most forcibly" by the different attitudes towards the two killers.

Israel Lipski

William Bury, 1889

A wife murderer – one of many that Berry was called upon to hang in the course of his career – Bury was one man suspected of being the serial killer known as Jack the Ripper. Suspicion rested on the fact that like the Ripper victims, Bury's wife had been found with abdominal wounds on her body, and Bury had lived in Whitechapel throughout the period in which the murders were committed. There was even a rumour that he had confessed his identity to a police officer before his death, although this is disputed. Berry firmly believed that Bury was Jack the Ripper, a conviction he maintained until the end of his life.

Acknowledgements

My thanks go out to all those who have supported me in researching and putting together this book: my devoted beta readers and family, Eric, Maura and Sandra; my partner and assistant proofreader Mark; James and Megan at *The Local Leader* magazine for so kindly helping me with promotion, and the long-suffering staff at Bradford Local Studies Library for their many attempts to show me how to correctly load a microfilm!

Lisa Firth

November 2014

Bibliography

Books

- Baring-Gould, S. *Yorkshire Oddities, Incidents and Strange Events*, 1877
- Beale, R David, and Lee Van Den Daele, Richard. *Milner Field: the Lost Country House of Titus Salt Jnr*, 2011
- Berry, James. *My Experiences as an Executioner*, 1892
- Berry, James. *The Hangman's Thoughts Above the Gallows*, 1905
- Campbell, Marie. *Strange World of the Brontës*, 2001
- Carpenter, Humphrey. *Tolkien: A Biography*, 1977
- Cudworth, William. *Histories of Bolton and Bowling*, 1891
- Doyle, Arthur Conan, et. al. *Princess Mary's Gift Book*, 1914
- Doyle, Arthur Conan. *The Coming of Fairies*, 1922
- Evans, Stewart P. *Executioner: Chronicles of a Victorian Hangman*, 2004.
- Fielding, Steve. *Pierrepoint: A Family of Executioners*, 2008
- Firth, Gary, and Hitt, Malcolm. *Bingley Past and Present*, 2009
- Forshaw, Chas F (ed.). *The Poets of Bingley, Keighley, Haworth and District*, 1891
- Gray, Johnnie. *Through Airedale from Goole to Malham*, 1891
- Green, Edward. *Prophet John Wroe: Virgins, Scandals and Visions in Victorian England*, 2013
- Griffiths, Frances, and Lynch, Christine. *Reflections on the Cottingley Fairies*, 2009
- Hall, Alan. *The Story of Bradford*, 2013
- Hansen, Astrid. *Wilsden*, 2001
- Hanson, Malcolm. *Keighley's Darkest Secrets*, 2010
- Kent, Alana. *"What's That Chimney Up There?"*, 1993
- Lister, Philip. *Ghosts & Gravestones of Haworth*, 2006
- Lockley, Philip. *Visionary Religion and Radicalism in Early Industrial England: From Southcott to Socialism*, 2012

- Markham, Leonard. *Tales of West Yorkshire*, 1992
- Newsam, William Cartwright. *The Poets of Yorkshire*, 1845
- Nicholson, John, and James, John. *The Poetical Works of John Nicholson with a Sketch of his Life and Writings*, 1859
- Nicholson, John. *Airedale in Ancient Times, Elwood and Elvina, the Poacher, and Other Poems*, 1824
- Petyt, KM. *Dialect and Accent in Industrial West Yorkshire*, 1985
- Scruton, William. *Pen and Pencil Pictures of Old Bradford*, 1890
- Speight, Harry. *Chronicles of Old Bingley*, 1898
- Turner, J Horsfall. *Ancient Bingley: or Bingley, its History and Scenery*, 1897
- Wade, Stephen. *Heroes, Villains and Victims of Bradford*, 2008
- Wade, Stephen. *Yorkshire Murders And Misdemeanours*, 2009
- Webb, Simon. *Execution: A History of Capital Punishment in Britain*, 2011
- Wright, Elizabeth Mary. *The Life of Joseph Wright: Vol. I*, 1932

Newspapers, magazines and journals

- Binns, Aethelbert (ed.). *Wilsden Almanac*. 1891
- Binns, Aethelbert (ed.). *Wilsden Almanac*. 1892
- Cooper, Joe. 'Cottingley: At Last the Truth'. *The Unexplained*. No. 117. pp. 2338-40. 1982
- Doyle, Arthur Conan. 'Fairies Photographed: An Epoch-making Event'. *The Strand Magazine*. Vol. 60. pp462-468. December 1920
- Doyle, Arthur Conan. 'The Evidence for Fairies'. *The Strand Magazine*. Vol. 61. pp199-206. June 1921
- Jones, Jonathan. 'The fake photographs that predate Photoshop'. *The Guardian*. 29 August 2012
- Kelly, Coral. 'An Appointment with the Hangman'. *Ripperologist* No. 18, August 1998
- Lunnon, Jenny. 'From woollen mills to dreaming spires'. *Oxford Mail*. 28 February 2008
- Miller, Russell. 'Sherlock Holmes and the curious case of the garden fairies'. *Daily Mail*. 15 October 2008
- Priestly, Mike. 'The Wright way to get on in life...'. *Bradford Telegraph and Argus*. 18 February 2008
- Sladen, Chris. 'Idle scholar who brought local language to book'. *Oxford Today*. 2010
- 'End of a Fairytale'. *Bradford Telegraph and Argus*. 1983
- *Bradford Observer*. 20 April 1843; 31 December 1857; 7 January 1858
- *Bradford Telegraph and Argus*. 19 April 1927
- *Burnley Express*. 5 July 1922; 6 September 1924

- *Huddersfield Chronicle, The.* 16 January 1858; 20 March 1858
- *Hull Packet and East Riding Times, The.* 1 January 1858; 15 January 1858
- *Keighley News.* 21 April 1927
- *Leeds Intelligencer, The.* 24 January 1828; 1 May 1858; 17 April 1858; 2 January 1858; 20 March 1858; 23 January 1858; 24 April 1858; 27 March 1858; 3 April 1858; 6 November 1858
- *Leeds Mercury, The.* 16 January 1858; 18 March 1858; 2 January 1858; 20 March 1858; 21 January 1858; 23 January 1858; 27 March 1858; 31 December 1857; 5 January 1858
- *Leeds Times.* 14 July 1883
- *Nottingham Evening Post.* 25 November 1920
- *Sheffield and Rotherham Independent* (supplement). 16 January 1858; 20 March 1858
- *Sheffield Independent.* 2 January 1858
- *Sunderland Daily Echo and Shipping Gazette.* 2 September 1922
- *York Herald, The.* 2 January 1858; 20 March 1858; 23 January 1858
- *Yorkshire Evening Post.* 14 March 1928; 18 February 1926; 19 April 1927; 28 January 1921; 28 June 1923; 5 October 1932
- *Yorkshire Gazette.* 13 March 1858; 16 January 1858; 2 January 1858; 23 January 1858; 6 March 1858
- *Yorkshire Post and Leeds Intelligencer.* 14 June 1922; 15 March 1928; 16 February 1929; 17 September 1932; 20 April 1927; 24 July 1922; 25 April 1923; 4 December 1928; 4 July 1923

Web-based sources

- bolling.net. Bolling Family Association website
- news.bbc.co.uk/1/hi/entertainment/1218778.stm. BBC News, 13 March 2001: '"Fairy" pictures fetch £6,000'
- news.bbc.co.uk/1/hi/uk/134243.stm. BBC News, 16 July 1998: '"Fairy" fakes sell for fortune'
- vcp.e2bn.org/case_studies/casestudy11906-information-on-arsenic-and-testing-for-arsenic-poisoning-reports-page.html. Victorian Crime & Punishment (information on arsenic poisoning)
- www.bbc.co.uk/bradford/sense_of_place/unexplained/cottingley_fairies.shtml. BBC, Spring 2004: 'Next stop, Fairyland!'
- www.bradfordhistorical.org.uk/antiquary/second/vol09/nicholson.html. The Bradford Antiquary: Unpublished Poems of John Nicholson
- www.britannica.com/EBchecked/topic/36303/arsenic-poisoning. *Encyclopaedia Britannica* website (information on arsenic poisoning)
- www.capitalpunishmentuk.org: Capital Punishment UK website
- www.classicsandclass.info. 'Classics and Class in Britain (1789-1939)',

an AHRC-funded research project
- www.cottingleyconnect.org.uk. Cottingley Connect (Cottingley village website)
- www.historyinanhour.com/2012/09/04/the-cottingley-fairies-summary. 'The Cottingley Fairies: a summary'
- www.medicinenet.com/arsenic_poisoning/article.htm. MedicineNet (information on arsenic poisoning)
- www.saltairevillage.info. Saltaire Village World Heritage Site website
- www.siracd.com/life_father.shtml. 'Charles Altamont Doyle – The Father of Arthur Conan Doyle'
- www.thelocalleader.org.uk: The Local Leader (Bradford magazine)
- www.umilta.net/SirJamesRoberts.html. 'Sir James Roberts and Saltaire' (a family history)
- www.workhouses.org.uk/Keighley. The Workhouse: the story of an institution (information on Exley Head workhouse)

Historical records
- 1851 England Census
- 1861 England Census
- 1871 England Census
- 1881 England Census
- 1891 England Census
- 1901 England Census
- 1911 England Census
- England & Wales, Death Index, 1916-2007
- England & Wales, FreeBMD Death Index, 1837-1915
- England & Wales, FreeBMD Marriage Index, 1837-1915
- England, Select Births and Christenings, 1538-1975
- England, Select Marriages, 1538-1973
- Miscellaneous records and literature held by the West Yorkshire Archive Service
- West Yorkshire, England, Baptisms, Marriages and Burials, 1512-1812
- West Yorkshire, England, Births and Baptisms, 1813-1910
- West Yorkshire, England, Deaths and Burials, 1813-1985

List of Photographs and Illustrations

Images credited as "public domain" are outside UK copyright, as the creator has been dead for over 70 years or, where no creator is identified, images are above 70 years old. Every attempt has been made to obtain reprint permission for copyrighted images used. If you believe your copyright has unintentionally been infringed, please contact the author on lisa@lisafirtheditorial.co.uk. She will be happy to come to an arrangement for future reprints of this title.

- Cover: Milner Field c. 1885 (public domain)
- p(iii): Claude Shepperson fairy illustration (public domain)
- p(iv): Map of Bradford and Airedale (© OpenStreetmap contributors)
- p(vi) (top): Salts Mill, 1859 (public domain)
- p(vi) (bottom): Salts Mill as it is today (© Mark Jankowski via Wikimedia Commons)
- p1: Sir Titus Salt (public domain)
- p4: Saltaire Congregational Church (© Lisa Firth)
- p7: Saltaire lion (© Lisa Firth)
- p9: Trafalgar Square lion (© Jose L. Marin via Wikimedia Commons)
- p10: Titus Salt Jr (public domain)
- p11: Milner Field house (public domain)
- p12: The Royal Couple visit Milner Field, June 1882 (public domain)
- p13: Official Programme for the Royal Visit to Bradford, June 1882 (public domain)
- p14 (top): Milner Field conservatory (public domain)
- p14 (bottom): Milner Field conservatory floor today (© Lisa Firth)
- p16 (top): Detail from Milner Field bay window (public domain)
- p16 (bottom): Milner Field window rubble (© Lisa Firth)
- p18: Milner Field library, 1885 (public domain)
- p22: John Nicholson by William Overend Geller (public domain)
- p24: View over Hewenden Valley (© Lisa Firth)
- p32 (top): Bingley Parish Church (© Lisa Firth)
- p32 (bottom): Grave of Mary Nicholson, nee Driver (© Lisa Firth)
- p36 (top): Postcard of Goit Stock, 1909 (public domain)
- p36 (bottom): View of Goit Stock Waterfall (© Lisa Firth)
- p38 (top): Goit Stock Mill tearooms (photographer unknown; believed public domain)
- p38 (bottom): Goit Stock Mill dancehall (photographer unknown; believed public domain)
- p39: Wreckage of Goit Stock Mill, left, and remains of musical

instruments, right (public domain)

Printed in Great Britain
by Amazon

38087617R00069